Deadly Route

Anne Varner
Karen DeVanie

Publishing Assistance Provided by:

Michelle Morrow, M.S.

Deadly Route

Karen DeVanie

Anne Varner

Book Two of the Say My Name Series

Inspired by True Events

Our hearts go out to anyone adversely affected by the events revealed in this story. We respect that murder ripples through families, friends, and communities, leaving permanent scars. The retelling of this case is an attempt to bring darkness to light and enable healing.

One: Georgia

I'M RUNNING for my life and then without warning the ground below me disappears.

The air is violently yanked from my lungs by an invisible, aggressive vacuum. My chest tightens as if someone dropped an anvil on me. The whoosh of escaping oxygen echoes in my ears.

Pure panic pulses through my body as I battle against gravity, clawing at the air for anything to stop me from being siphoned into a dark abyss. My arms are flailing, and my heartbeat bangs like a bass drum. I'm falling—too fast, too hard. Quicker than breath. Faster than thought. The ground erupts beneath me like an explosion in reverse. I jolt upright, breathless, muscles as tight as steel cables. But I already know what this is.

I've had this nightmare a million times. These

dreams are products of stressful situations; before my first ballet recital, the night before I took my SATs in high school and every day for the first week of college.

Momma always told me my dreams were a manifestation of my fear of failure. She would tease me and say, "If you believe in yourself the dreams will stop."

What if it's not a dream this time?

Why now—in the middle of the day—does it feel so real? There's something distinctly peculiar about this dream. It's not symbolic. This is combat. Real. Raw. Visceral. I'm under attack.

The weight of my assailant's body on top of me lets me know this nightmare is worse than usual. The crash of the hard ground didn't wake me this time.

His odor fills my senses. Acrid. Charred. Sour. Rusty.

The dankness of the soil mixed with the humidity of June in southeastern Virginia wafts past me. A primal scream tears through me as I run. I can't discern if the shriek is mine or his. I turn around to detect the direction of the sound and see a heap of bodies writhing in the dirt.

The assailant is stabbing his victim. She's screaming. A gut-wrenching, soul-ripping scream that slices through the air like a serrated blade.

My instinct is to run and save her. Then the worst realization of all crashes in:

The girl isn't her. She's me.

A void of deafening silence closes in, rendering me motionless. Stillness floods in like a tsunami, swallowing every sound, every flicker of light.

He killed me.

Two: Georgia

S UDDENLY, I'm in my mom's kitchen. My hair is wet. I am wearing a pair of jeans and a comfy flannel over my favorite Lynyrd Skynyrd t-shirt.

My memory is familiar. My soul knows this scene by heart. I am a high school Junior and getting ready to go on a camping trip with my friends. Momma hums as she packs peanut butter sandwiches, sliding them into sandwich bags with practiced hands. The smell of her homemade bread mixes with the citrusy remnants of my shampoo. The warmth of her love wraps me in a comforting hug. We're joking and laughing. Mom is making bets on how long I'll last in the wilderness without the comforts of home. Her laughter ricochets off the cabinets and spins through the sunbeams slanting across the linoleum. It bounces off every surface and lands right in my heart. She entices me by offering up a homemade chocolate cake if I stay the entire weekend without leaving. Challenge accepted!

I lean in to kiss her soft cheek and I hear a whooshing sound as I'm sucked from this soothing scene.

I'm falling again. Being dragged from breath, from gravity, from momma. From everything that ever made sense. I'm hurtling backward through a stark white arctic tunnel, faster than thought or time—then slam —I'm dropped straight into my high school graduation ceremony.

Now I'm standing on a football field under an oppressive June sun, suffocating in a gold cap and gown that I absolutely abhor. Who thought it was a good idea to dress the girls in this hideous color that looks exactly like a mustard packet? From the view of the stands, we must resemble walking condiments. The boys are in burgundy, the girls in gold—ketchup and mustard. We look more like we're getting ready to dress a hot dog instead of graduating from high school.

Ever since the cap and gown were delivered, Dad has been relentless. Every morning it's a new nickname: "Grey Poupon," "French's," "Honey Mustard,"

"Gouldens." He even called me "Deli" over pancakes last weekend, as if I was a sandwich order. Mom eggs him on with her incessant cackling which only fuels his creativity.

In the audience, I spot Momma. She's holding a bouquet of white roses, a silent protest against the school colors because she knows how much I hate them. The green of the stems and the soft ivory petals resemble relish and onions from a distance, our little inside joke. I catch her eye and she smiles, and we both dissolve into giggles.

It's surreal to think that in just a few months, I'll be leaving her, leaving home, for college. I'm not sure how to describe what she means to me. Mom isn't just a parent, she's my mirror, my safe place. She sees the me no one else notices. She always says she fell in love with me the moment she knew she was pregnant. I think I fell in love with her the second I saw her face. Dad is the anchor that keeps our family grounded, but Mom is the lifeline that keeps me afloat. She's been my North Star, unwavering, steady, always there to light the way when I get lost. I've told her things I've never said out loud to anyone else. We're not just mother and daughter, we're pieces of the same soul orbiting each other.

Then, the moment comes. Tassels shift from right

to left, a synchronized sweep of fabric and time, and just like that, we're graduates. I catch the shimmer of a tear sliding down Momma's cheek, a proud, quiet glisten that breaks me wide open.

Then, another WHOOSH, and I'm falling again.

Three: Olive

I READ Toby's facial expression as soon as I am on the school bus. There's a volatile electricity in the air that seems to pulse with each turn of the bus wheels. I can feel it settle like static along my arms, a sixth sense warning me that Toby is slipping, one slow degree at a time, into a version of himself I fear and barely recognize.

He is sitting in the back alone, jaw clenched, red faced, body visibly tense. His fingernails dig into his jeans as though he's holding something inside that's clawing to get out. His leg bounces in an erratic rhythm, a visible metronome of the chaos ticking through his veins. I am expecting a pressure cooker back there and know before I take one step down the aisle that a Toby storm is brewing. Toby's volatility is like gasoline, and I'm holding the match.

Toby was chipper all day, despite being in the middle of exams. I saw him at lunchtime in the courtyard cutting up and rough housing with the guys. Joking around with his hysterical one-liners. That was the Toby who made you forget how fast he could turn.

He hasn't spoken to me since I canceled our plans, but his silence is louder than anything he could say. It echoes, building pressure, waiting to break. His shoulders are rigid as steel, and he's radiating something dark and dangerous. The kind of mood that doesn't just sour the air, it infects it. You can feel it crawling across the bus seats like smoke, stinging eyes and touching nerves.

Toby's moods don't just shift, they build and snap. A slow coiling begins behind his eyes. A film seems to drop over his face, dulling his features into something slack and foreign. He doesn't blink. He just watches the world go by with a hollow stare, as if he's measuring how close he is to the edge.

He can be intimidating. It's not so much his size, but more his drastic mood swings. He has an average build for a Junior in high school. His strength is what we refer to as farm strong. Although he lifts weights for athletics, he is far from a muscle-bound weightlifter.

I dread Toby's sullen mood, especially knowing I put him there. Earlier in the week, we agreed to go to the county library today after school to study for the upcoming Geometry exam. At lunch, Alyssa told me a bunch of our girlfriends are gathering at the country club pool until dinner time. Setting my social priorities, I canceled my study plans with Toby. He didn't say anything when I told him. Disappointment was etched in the dark stones of his eyes and I chose to ignore it. Now his black aura is filling the bus, encircling the students in a cloak of agitation. The entire bus of students feels his aggravation and they avoid him, whether consciously or instinctively, I'm not sure. A third grader is clutching his lunchbox as if it's a flotation device. A middle school girl subtly moves her backpack between her and Toby, creating a makeshift wall. Nobody says anything. Nobody dares. The weight of Toby's mood has made everyone a hostage.

There are less jokes, and everyone steers clear of the electric fence of rage surrounding his seat. I might be the only one who can defuse him. It's up to me to protect the other students, especially the younger ones, who may not recognize the warning signs.

I suck in a slow breath and force a smile, rehearsing my lines, a performer stepping onto a hostile stage. There are no open seats near Toby, only with him, but I am neither brave nor stupid enough to drop onto the bench next to him in these moments. He requires a wide berth.

The bus continues its route toward the end of the ride and the seats start to empty. I twist myself around in an attempt to catch his eye. His brown wavy hair is unkempt from the heat and humidity of the day. The sun has brought out his freckles which gives his skin a dirty appearance. His small brown eyes are fixated in a glare out the window as the bus chugs along rural back roads. I marvel at how he seemingly stares at one thing while the rest of the world passes by. Is he immune to motion- sickness?

After a couple of waves of my hands, his attention breaks from the imaginary target of his fixation. Toby cuts his eyes toward me. I plaster a smile upon my face, hoping it's friendly enough for him to take the bait. I motion for him to come closer and ask if he is aware of what Earl did to Alyssa in science class as school was ending. Of course, I knew the story. According to Toby, he too is up to speed about the antics. I ask him to come and tell me, pretending I am not privy to the details of the high jinks between the two students. I figure if I can get him to recount the funny story, his concentration will be distracted from my transgression of breaking our plans which seems to be gripping his mind. Maybe his anger will subside in the telling of the story, therefore saving any unsuspecting bus rider from setting Toby off and suffering his wrath. Finally, Toby moves toward the front of the bus and joins me in my seat. Stop after stop, the bus continues to empty. Toby and I continue to guffaw at the funny events of the day; it's a great stress reliever.

As more students offload from the bus, Toby's temperament lifts as if each kid carries away a bit of his furious dark cloud. Finally, the bus is empty except for me, Toby, and a second- grade girl named Lexi who is seated in front of us. Her bespectacled face is framed with blonde pigtails and rosy cheeks. Lexi will be dropped off right before Toby and then I'm the last student on the bus's afternoon route.

Although Lexi started the school year sheepish and introverted, she is beginning to come out of her shell and interact occasionally with the other students. I enjoy sitting alongside the second grader in the mornings because Lexi doesn't usually engage in much conversation before 10AM and neither do I.

In the mornings, her wide green eyes quietly steal coy glances of the upper classmen passengers. In the afternoons, Lexi is more animated. I see her giggle at the funny antics around her, although she still doesn't have much to say.

On this particular afternoon, Lexi is seated in the front seat, with Toby and me in the row directly behind her. After Toby finishes telling me about Alyssa and Earl, we recount our school day: the exams we took, our grade predictions, and which exams are scheduled for tomorrow.

Lexi turns and rests her chin on the back of her seat, curiously watching us and listening to our conversation. For reasons unknown, Toby interprets this action as an encroachment on his privacy. He glares at her through clenched teeth and growls for her to turn around. Toby's recoiling back into his mood catches me off guard. Fun Toby disappears and Dark Toby replaces him without warning. I attempt to diffuse the situation by jovially stating the little girl is watching me and not looking at him.

Toby blurts out, "I don't give a shit who she's looking at! She don't need to be turning round and gettin' in our business."

With a jolt, Lexi snaps back to face the front of the bus. The heat of embarrassment mixed with fear radiates from her little head. I remind Toby she is a harmless little girl and to watch his salty language. I scramble to say something funny to trigger a calmer disposition from Toby. Reaching deep into my arsenal, I extract something tried and true that always worked on him in the past. I remind him how our kooky English teacher, Ms. Ross, once again wore two completely different shoes to school earlier in the week. I hurriedly describe each shoe, demonstrating with my fingers how they had different height heels. I laugh, saying "Who doesn't realize you are wearing one shoe taller than the other?" This dialogue seems to pull Toby back into the light as he giggles his snorty laugh.

We try to count the times Ms. Ross attended school with all kinds of wardrobe faux pas throughout our high school years. This is a running point of humor for the class, especially since the English teacher's son is a classmate.

Immersed in our conversation, I fail to discern Lexi sneaking to face us, her chin perched on her knuckles, her fingers curled and gripping the edge. Unexpectedly, Toby's fist lands on the back of the seat so close to Lexi's fingers, I am not sure if he actually struck them or not.

I shriek as if I myself am hit.

Lexi freezes and her little eyes well with tears. I shout, "What the hell is wrong with you!?"

Toby answers sharply, "Yeah, you little bitch, what the hell is wrong with you?"

My hand flies to cover my mouth and I gasp. The

scene is chaotic. I want to jump the seat to console the little girl, but I'm frozen.

Toby lands another lightning-fast punch. This time he undeniably directs his attack right onto Lexi's tiny pink fingers, still curled around the back of the seat. Lexi lets out a terrified yelp and snatches her fingers back.

Pure rage emanates from Toby, shifting the earth off- kilter. Reactively, I seize Toby's arm to ward off another attack on the child. Getting right into Toby's face, something I have never done before, I implore him to stop this craziness. The red in his eyes cuts through me like lasers. Assuming he cannot hear me, I scream in his face, not knowing what kind of reaction I'll receive. "TOBY! TOBY!"

His focus abruptly changes, and our eyes connect as if he suddenly sees and hears me through the veil of his ire. Yanking his arm out of my grip, he turns his back on me and once again glares through the window, blood red rage radiating from him.

Thankfully, we arrive at Lexi's stop next. The little girl runs off the bus, not stopping until she reaches her door. Stunned by the whole situation, I miss the opportunity to make sure she's okay.

The bus driver's eyes meet mine in the large rearview mirror as time stands still. We stare at each other's reflection, but then Mr. Railey breaks eye contact and gets the bus under way. Because Mr. Railey has been our bus driver for the past five years, he has observed his share of Toby's outbursts and mood swings. Although he might report this to the school administration, he chooses not to physically confront Toby on the bus. For the following ten minutes the bus bounces along the country road in complete silence.

Toby has utterly shut down.

Try as I might, I cannot make words form in my mouth. I can't even construct a sentence in my brain. What happened? In the six years of my knowing Toby, I have never seen him go to this extreme. Occasionally I catch him tripping kids or nudging them off balance as they board or unboard the bus, seemingly for sport. But this?

This is next level.

He assaulted Lexi for looking his way. He physically harmed her without one iota of remorse or second guessing what he did.

The bus slows at Toby's driveway.

I ease myself into the aisle and stand with my back to him enabling his departure. Toby pushes his way out of the seat, his shoulder making a directed thud against my back, knocking me off balance. As he stands on the bottom step, he waits for the bus to stop and the driver to open the door. Without a word or a glance in my direction, Toby leaves me there in stunned silence.

And I wonder: who was that?

Who is this dark passenger that lives at the edge of my friend... my classmate... my neighbor? And how long has it been waiting to come out?

Four: Olive

L EAVING A NOTE on the kitchen counter letting my parents know where I went, I glide into my prized possession, the 1972 hunter green Buick my grandfather handed down to me on my 16th birthday. The white velour seats make the back of my legs turn into a puddle in the summer heat, but it's mine, and I love it unconditionally. I never use the A/C until July because I treasure the feeling of the wind in my hair as I blast the radio—my radio. I don't share my control over the tunes with anyone!

I was elated when Grampy gave me those keys. I practically jumped into his arms. I happily accepted the stipulations handed down with the car: I will still ride the bus until my Senior year, no more than two passengers at a time, and my weekend curfew is 10PM and 7PM on weekdays.

Today it's just me and the Buick on the open road as I drive to meet my friends. I wave at our mail lady as I make my way to the country club. She and I are the only ones on the road. As our cars pass, I can hear the band Boston blasting from her station wagon.

"This is freedom!" I shout out the window as my hair blows in the wind.

I love lounging by the pool in the warm summer heat. The sound of swimmers splashing as they jump off the diving board into the water makes my heart happy. The aroma of pool chlorine and the coconut from my tanning oil form a perfume that permeates my soul. I find my friends lounging in chairs facing the action. I take my seat at the end, kick off my flip flops, and smooth my crisp beach towel along the top of the hot plastic seat. I plop onto my lounger, gripping an ice-cold TAB cola in my hand. Laying the headrest back in the perfect position, I'm propped up just enough to see the action in the pool but low enough to stretch my long slender body and cross my feet at the ankles.

Puffy white clouds crawl across an azure sky. A whiff of fresh, hot fries wafts from the screened porch attached to the country club restaurant and tickles my nose, making my stomach rumble. My mirrored sunglasses allow me to peek at the cute boys in the pool without being too obvious. I recognize some familiar faces but none who excite me enough to take my attention away from the hot gossip my friends are divulging. I am craving relaxation because this day seems never-ending.

I'm counting the hours until school ends for the summer. After three more days, I'll officially be a Senior.

I can hear Alyssa ranting over her boyfriend Earl and the trouble he's in after a prank he and his friends pulled during science class. Something about a Bunsen burner and Alyssa's diary.

The Steve Miller Band belts out Abracadabra on a staticky radio station somewhere on the other side of the pool.

I lean back and close my eyes as Alyssa recounts her side of the same story Toby described to me on our tumultuous bus ride home. I'm still unsettled by Toby's rage. He's changed through the years. The first time I remember meeting him we were in fifth grade, and his name was Jeb, short for Jebidiah. I began attending Cottonwood Academy that year, which we call "The Academy," since it is the only private academy in our southeastern Virginia county. The school consists of three main buildings: one for elementary school (Pre- K through fourth grade), one for middle school (fifth through seventh grade), and one for high school (eighth through twelfth grade). Additionally, there is a library and a gymnasium which are utilized by all students.

Under 400 students currently attend The Academy. Ours is one of the largest classes, coming in at 42 kids. There is no cafeteria, but we love our little lunchroom and the open courtyard where we gather during breaks.

The lunchroom is basically a classroom converted by adding a Formica counter in the middle of the room. Along the walls are small vending machines offering cold sodas and snacks. Behind the counter stands the lunch lady, Mrs. Doughty, who reigns over several crock pots of barbeque and boiling red hot dogs, a few microwaves, a refrigerator, and a large chest-style freezer. If you want hot food, you place your order through Mrs. Doughty who lovingly pops your selection into the microwave and hands you a steaming plastic bag of whatever items you've purchased.

In the lower grades, teachers place lunch orders in the morning and the students are served and eat the meals in the classrooms before spilling onto the playground for lunch break. In high school, we cram into the small space, 20 kids at a time, making it nearly impossible to move, let alone circumvent the crowd and race your piping hot lunch outside to a cement table before you burn your hand off.

In the fifth grade, Jeb and I were appointed by our homeroom teacher to be the lunchroom order runners for our class. After she tallied the lunch selections and milk orders, we would walk together to Mrs. Doughty and hand in the class's lunch order. It was on these daily walks that we became fast friends. Being selected to this important job was a big deal, because we got to walk past the high school building and could peer into the windows of the upper classes.

I was selected because I was new to the school and the teacher believed the task would enable me to quickly remember the layout of the campus. Jeb was selected because he had attended The Academy since Pre-K and knew the layout by heart. Back then, we traveled on a buddy system to prevent students from getting lost on the campus. Generally, Jeb was a quiet kid, as was I, which is why we got along so well. We loved playing on the monkey bars at recess or watching the younger kids chase each other around the playground.

Like me, Jeb was not the smartest kid in our class but not the slowest. We were both average kids from average homes. We were nicely tucked into the middle of the pack. I learned a way of communicating with Jeb where no one else could manage. He developed a hair-trigger temper, but I cultivated an ability to placate him. Usually, I could tell him a joke or remind him of a funny story from our younger days of impulsive antics. Throughout the years my tactic worked and saved Jeb from getting into trouble.

By the seventh grade, refocusing his anger became more challenging. I remember one day in English class we read a story involving a farmer who owned slaves. The teacher picked different students to read the part of the farmer, his wife, and the slaves. The teacher gave Jeb the part of the slave named Rodney and he lost his mind. He turned red in the face, his hands started shaking, and his eyes turned as dark as I'd ever seen them. He flat-out refused to read the part. He furiously threw his book at the teacher and stomped from the classroom.

The whole class went deadly quiet, the teacher slumped at her desk, mouth agape. This was uncharted territory. We'd never seen a student throw a book at a teacher and I doubt the teacher had experienced such an event before.

Jeb got suspended from school for a couple of days. Upon his return, he seemed like my old friend. The rage was no longer in his eyes, but I could tell something was a little different. A crack had formed and couldn't be glued back together. A glimmer of anger simmered below the surface. Occasionally, Jeb's anger popped up whenever the boys in our class teased him by calling him Rodney. I always hated their taunting because Jeb's temper was rabid and red hot which made him unpredictable. Once his anger subsided outwardly, he would seethe over the teasing for days and obsess over exacting revenge one day. None of us believed he would unleash retaliation. We chalked it up to his quirky personality.

Eighth-grade year brought a big change. Jeb announced he was going by Toby now and not to call him Jeb anymore. Toby is his middle name therefore the name change wasn't completely unfounded. He grew taller and bulkier during the summer but still was one of the smallest boys in our class. He attributed his growth to playing a lot of baseball and spending more time running the neighborhood instead of watching TV or reading books. He began lifting weights in preparation for football season. The changes in his appearance and name did not disguise the rage still buried in his eyes. He seemed edgy all the time. Toby displayed big outbursts among other students at lunch and a couple times in gym class. Never anything as bad as the day in English class when he threw the book at the teacher, but enough to give us pause. We realized quickly the risks of pushing his buttons.

Our classmates learned to take a step back from Toby and walk on eggshells during his mood swings. Eighth grade was also the year we observed Toby following through on his threats of retaliation.

I am snapped from my memories by Miss Libby, the country club manager, calling my name: "Olive, sweetie, your mom called and asked me to tell you to head home right away because there's an emergency."

I bid my gal pals good-bye and, grabbing my towel, I trot to my car. While pulling on my coverup, I throw myself into my hot car and crank it up.

Five: Toby

A SAVAGE FORCE is living inside me coiled up, waiting to strike and I can feel it blooming and spreading roots deep into my soul, spreading like wildfire through bone and nerve. It's been there ever since I can remember. It's not new. A quiet tenant in the shadowed corners of my soul. But lately, it's grown brasher. Rougher. Eager.

I'm losing the battle to control it, and I don't mind. I prefer it to take control. If I'm being honest, I don't want to win. Because when The Savage takes control, I become something more than just a background blur. I am fire. I am thunder. I matter. People finally see me. They hear the edge in my voice and feel the heat of my stare. They flinch. They avoid. They obey.

Fear... it smells like copper and limes. Cleansing. Acidic. Gripping.

Whenever I pull back the curtain and let them get a glimpse of it pacing in its cage, their fear is palpable. That's when they respect me. Real, bone-deep, primal respect. The kind born from fear. In the moments The Savage is contained and silent, I'm just... Toby. The quiet one. The forgettable one.

And I hate him.

Generally, my friends see me as quiet, small, and meek. They chuckle behind my back and call me awkward. They assume my need for privacy and isolation equates to a lack of confidence. At times, the guys tease me about stuff I say or don't say. Even the teachers have a tone when they say my name. Like I'm dim. Like they feel sorry for the dull-eyed kid in the third row who never raises his hand and always turns his tests in early with answers scribbled too sloppy to read.

Don't even get me started on the girls in my class. I doubt they see me at all.

Some of them say I'm cute and quirky and they like those traits in a friend. The dreaded "Friend Zone." In the locker room, we call the Friend Zone "the pasture." That's where they put you out to graze when they've already decided you're never getting in the barn. And once you're there? Game over.

There was one time, in sophomore year, during a group presentation my fear of public speaking overcame me. I blanked out completely. The teacher called my name twice. I stood there with a poster in my hands, staring at the floor tiles like they were moving. My voice wouldn't work. My skin went cold. All I could hear was static in my ears and the sound of my own heartbeat—louder than anything else in the room. I don't remember sitting down. I don't remember what the teacher said. But I remember how they laughed. And I remember The Savage whispering to me, 'Weak.'

Last summer, at football practice I got in trouble for an illegal tackle against Rhett. What they didn't see was that Rhett called me Rodney under his breath after a play. My punishment for the illegal tackle, since it wasn't my first one, was to run extra laps in full gear. Coach held me back until the last car left the parking lot and then he released me. Not only was I going to be late for dinner, but I had a pile of homework waiting for me.

As I was driving home through the back roads, head buzzing, muscles sore, whole body crackling like a live wire. I was furious.

That's when I saw them.

I don't know if they noticed me, but I saw their faces in the reflection of the dashboard light of their car. I know they were laughing and talking about me.

And The Savage stirred.

He sneered: "You gonna let that slide? Those bitches are laughing at you."

I increased my speed, annoyed by their judgment. I flashed my lights at them as I rode their bumper.

The girls pulled to the side of the road, probably thinking I was a cop.

Good little girls, obedient in fear.

The Savage was oozing out of me as I approached the driver's window, my Buck knife hidden by my side. Familiar. Heavy. Comforting.

Feeling the beastly breath on the back of my neck, I heard The Savage's low husky growl as he whispered inside my head, "You mess with the bull, you get the horns."

I tapped the window using the tip of the knife. Just a gentle hello. The driver cranked her window halfway down her expression riddled with apprehension. The smell of their terror teased my senses and sent a rush of adrenaline through my veins. Like air before a lightning strike. It was intoxicating. The driver's fearful eyes were darting back and forth as the passenger stared into the abyss outside the windshield. Finally, the three of us locked eyes as The Savage lunged with a roar and unleashed his power with a spring. The urge to wrap my calloused white hands around their delicate black throats seared my brain.

The bitch quickly locked her door as I reached for the handle and brought the knife through her window. I landed a slash across her shoulder, fast and fluid motion rewarding my senses. Both bitches screamed as the driver floored the gas pedal and screeched tires out of there.

The momentum nearly knocked me on my ass. Almost eating gravel, I stumbled back to my car and cackled, "Y'all will always be the ones who got away." I reveled in my car, belly laughing for a good ten minutes before I headed home.

But later that night, back in my bedroom, staring into the ceiling fan as it spun overhead, I slipped out of myself again. The silence was too much. My mind clicked off. I don't remember how long I laid there. Minutes? Hours? I just remember blinking and realizing the knife was still in my hand. My skin buzzed for hours. My brain for days. The adrenaline high from the hunt lasted for weeks boosting my confidence. I looked people in the eye with my newfound cockiness. Because they didn't know what I'd done. But I did. And so did The Savage

Six: Georgia

WHOOSH... AGAIN, I'm yanked through the tunnel, spinning backward at light-speed, the cold pressing in like invisible hands. The icy nothingness swallows me whole.

And then, just as suddenly, I land in the fluorescent-lit cafeteria of Blueridge College, seated with my dorm mates at our usual spot, the back corner table, half-forgotten by the rest of the world. The air is thick with the smell of dread: liver, onions, and fried okra. It assaults my nose the moment I sit down, like a punishment you can't outrun. It's the same every time, as if the cooks are trying to gaslight our taste buds into submission.

As if to make up for this culinary cruelty, the cafeteria ladies always serve chocolate cake on liver night. But this? This thing on my tray is no cake. It's a crime scene.

The slice in front of me is somehow both brittle and soggy. I think it forgot what it wanted to be halfway through baking. The cake part clearly came from a generic box mix, dry as sandpaper, and the icing is just Sunday's leftover chocolate pudding lazily spooned on top. They didn't even try to disguise it. It's a sad slab of cafeteria propaganda pretending to be dessert.

Chocolate cake is supposed to be comfort. Love. Home.

This monstrosity? It's punishment for some collective student sin we weren't even aware we committed. Do they think we won't recognize the pudding from Sunday dinner, now sitting limply on this overcooked sponge? As if we'd forget. I take one bite and instantly regret it, my homesickness crashes into me like a rogue wave.

God, I miss Momma's cake.

The memory of her glistening, triple-layer chocolate masterpiece hits me full force. Moist, rich, and coated in her signature 7-minute frosting that melts on your tongue, finished with delicate chocolate shavings like confetti from the heavens. Momma bakes with soul. With intention. Her cake is an experience and pure magic in a pan. After just one week away, I'd walk the ninety miles home barefoot if it meant getting a slice.

One afternoon, I finally call her. I pretend I'm just checking in, but we both know I'm homesick, unraveling at the edges. Her voice is warm and I clutch the phone like a lifeline.

"I keep having that dream again," I whisper, eyes stinging. "The one where something's chasing me, and I fall."

Momma doesn't miss a beat. "That's your self-doubt talking again, baby. You always have that dream when you're feeling unsure."

Her calm seeps through the receiver like medicine. She reminds me of who I am and reminds me to trust myself. To give it time.

Then, she issues a challenge, like only she can. "Make it to Thanksgiving without coming home, and I'll have a whole chocolate cake waiting just for you."

My heart clenches, but I grin. "Challenge accepted."

I wait for her laugh, the one that always bubbles up right after I say those words. But instead, WHOOSH.

The tunnel drags me under again.

Seven: Georgia

I MEET MACK in my Senior year of college. Having relinquished my participation in the band, I am now free to roam the stadium and soak in the fall air during football games. That's when it happens, leaving the concession booth, I walk straight into him, clumsily sloshing my Coke all over his flannel shirt.

Instantly, we both notice we're wearing nearly identical outfits. His flannel flanks a Molly Hatchet tee, mine rests over my favorite Lynyrd Skynyrd shirt. The coincidence feels like a scene written just for us. We laugh hard and in that moment, something shifts in the atmosphere.

His laugh is deep and easy. My cheeks ache from smiling. He asks if I'd like to grab food after the game. I flash him a grin, saying, "Why wait until after the game if I'm hungry now?"

My voice comes out lighter than usual. I hear flirtatious, playful tones as I speak. Who is this version of me? We slowly make our way to his truck, avoiding distractions from our conversation. We make an instant connection, as if we'd known each other for years although we'd met by chance. Mack's sun-kissed freckles, tousled sandy blonde hair, and toned farm-boy build make it hard to concentrate. I can feel my stomach doing somersaults.

We stop at a faded maroon and white 1968 Ford Highboy which seems to have seen better days. Grass stains discolor the white stripes and a rusty dent in the tailgate highlight rugged years of farm use. It's nothing fancy, and yet I love the workhorse of a truck immediately as if it were a dear cousin. There's something honest about it. Something honest about Mack.

He opens the door for me as I question how in the world, I will gracefully hoist myself into this monster truck? I grip the seat belt and lift myself, hoping for the best. He chuckles while apologetically telling me he is working two jobs trying to save for an upgrade, one perhaps lower to the ground. "Something better for my vertically-challenged passengers," he says, and then he winks. I swear my knees turn to limp spaghetti.

He drives us to the local Char Grill. The sparsely populated restaurant, thanks to the ongoing game, seems intimately quiet. We find a booth and get lost in conversation over burgers and shakes. The football fans begin spilling into the restaurant as we stand to leave. In that moment I pray we aren't recognized by any of the patrons, because selfishly I don't want our connection to be interrupted.

Mack navigates his truck back to the football field, now empty except for a handful of people cleaning up trash. He parks beside my car. Mack lowers his tailgate and we sit with our knees brushing, fingers eventually lacing together. We stay that way until long after midnight, saying everything and nothing and feeling the warmth of our hands clasped together.

I make my way back to my dorm close to 1:00AM. Giddy and light- headed, I worry I might wreck my car. If I'd known someone like Mack was hanging out at our football games, I would have quit the band sooner.

Momma suspects something is askew because I suddenly stop coming home every weekend, using the excuse of Senior projects. We both know she's too smart for that. She teases me, "Now do these projects include boys wearing ball caps and flannel?"

She knows me too well, so why deny it.

By Christmas break, I am ready to introduce Mack to my parents. I'm excited to divulge to them he grew up a mere twenty minutes away from me. I rehearse the words in my mirror, practicing how I'll casually introduce him to my curious family and friends. His dad is a farmer and his mom is a part-time secretary at the local bank. Mack's dad sent him to school for the 'college experience' before he steps into his position as the head of the family farm.

As a large animal veterinarian major, Mack has no intentions of being a vet, but he wants the knowledge to better care for the livestock on the farm. He's gotten plenty of agricultural experience from his dad through the years. The man grew up knee-deep in dirt and responsibility, and I admire the hell out of him for it. As a matter of fact, I find it downright sexy!

My parents are pleased as punch to meet him. It is evident Momma approves because she makes him one of her famous chocolate cakes the next day. The moment I share the dessert I've guarded like treasure all my life, I know I'm in love. I've found a cake-worthy man.

Time skips like a pebble across a glassy lake. One minute it's January and we are building a snowman then suddenly we are preparing for our college graduation. At the ceremony Mack crosses the stage to receive his diploma and I'm not sure who cheers louder, my parents or his. Ten minutes later, as I step from the stage, diploma in hand, I spy Mack on bended knee. Right there in the middle of the ceremony he proposes, and my classmates and family erupt into cheers. I don't remember saying yes, but I do remember tears, applause, and my heart screaming "Finally!" What a magical moment!

We marry in a small ceremony the following spring and move into a small house on his family's property. The house is the same one his parents moved into when they first bought the farm. The farmhouse is small but charming and suits us perfectly. The warn paneled walls hum with stories of generations, and now they get to embrace ours too.

Mack finally buys a car: a used deep blue Pontiac Trans Am. It's bold and sexy and beautiful! He had used the majority of his savings from his two jobs on my engagement ring, leaving him little left for a car.

I love my ring, but I adore the Trans Am. I drive the beauty on the weekends but during the week I drive my dad's old clunker station wagon he donated to me in college.

The car is more suitable for my mail route. It's beat up, but reliable, and holds all my mail crates and parcels for the rural route I've started. It smells like worn vinyl and coffee. It purrs like an old man with a cold in winter.

The station wagon is where I will meet my agonizing death.

My heart flutters at the thought. I don't know why. Maybe some part of me senses it. The stillness that will follow. The kind of silence that comes after a hurricane or a tornado. First the violence of a storm, then a tangible quietness. Maybe this is the moment I'm supposed to remember. Mack. The laughter. The love. The cake. The WHOOSH.

Eight: Toby

I KNOW I'm in trouble before I even step through the front door. I'm late for supper, and tonight was my turn to set the table.

Mom's anger hangs in the air like a summer storm, charged and ready to strike. By the time she catches me tiptoeing through the family room, trying to disappear down the hallway to my bedroom, her temper has already boiled over.

Our house is small, just one story of cramped brick and tension. The layout is simple: three bedrooms at the back, an eat-in kitchen and family room at the front. Mom has decorated the living space with blue floral wallpaper and a shag carpet to match, like she's trying to make the place cozier than it wants to be. The wood-paneled hallway is cluttered with family pictures of forced smiles frozen in time, watching as I pass.

My room is first on the right, Keith's is across the hall next to the bathroom we share, and my parents' room is at the very end. Their door is always shut, but the thin walls offer no secrets. Some nights, they're screaming like enemies; others, they're tangled in whispers and breathless murmurs. There's never a middle ground. Just war or worship.

The smell of pot roast and potatoes clings to every surface of the house. As I'm halfway down the hall, Mom's voice slices through the silence: sharp and commanding. "Turn around. You're joining us at the table."

When I finally slide into my chair, I notice everyone's already started eating. Before I can even sit fully, Dad gives me a hard look and jerks his chin toward the hallway. "Wash your hands," he mutters, disappointed. "You know better."

I return to find my plate empty. Mom doesn't say a word at first, just shoots me a glare and nods at the pot roast. "Serve yourself," she says flatly. "We'll talk about your behavior after dinner." I smirk to myself. Good. I prefer serving my own plate anyway.

The rest of the meal is silent, thick with tension. No one makes eye contact. When we finish, I start to rise, but Mom stops me mid-motion. "You're doing the dishes," she snaps. "Since Keith had to set the table again because you were late. Again."

I swear this woman is obsessed with the word "again." And now she has me saying it. Again. Again. Again. I don't protest. I don't care.

Once my chores are done, I escape to my room and shut the door behind me like sealing off a pressure chamber. I flick on my stereo, lie back on my single bed, and let the distorted guitar riffs swallow me whole.

This room is mine. It's not much, but it's my sanctuary. The walls, once white, are now papered with Black Sabbath and AC/DC posters, their faded colors clashing with the rust-colored carpet that hides more grime than I'd ever admit. My curtains are brown and plaid, thick enough to keep the room in near-perpetual dusk, the way I like it. Every month, Mom replaces the bulbs in my ceiling light, thinking she's helping. Every month, I unscrew one just to maintain the dim vibe.

Behind the door hangs my most prized possession: Farrah Fawcett in her red bathing suit, lips parted just so. Her eyes follow me around the room like she's watching my every move. Sometimes I wonder if she sees what I'm becoming.

I toss a baseball into the air and catch it with a

satisfying smack of leather on skin. The rhythm calms me. The repetition feels like control.

Bang! Mom barges in, planting herself at the edge of my bed, hands on hips. I barely glance at her.

She starts in, voice shrill and full of that grating disappointment. It's the second time this week I've been late for dinner. I'm falling behind on chores. She's "had enough." Blah, blah, blah.

Her words scrape against my brain like a fork on glass. How does Dad stand this every day? Her needling. Her endless griping. She bursts into my room like she owns it, like my space is hers to invade.

I want her gone.

I sit up, cock my head, and give her a cold glare. I say nothing. Just stare. My hand continues its rhythm: ball, glove, ball, glove. My rage simmers quietly beneath the surface, and I imagine driving the ball into her face, watching it connect. I know exactly how to throw it. The perfect release. Clean. Devastating. I'm a pitcher, after all.

The thought thrills me. She finally turns to leave, muttering under her breath. Just before she crosses the threshold, I hurl the ball.

WHACK.

It hits her square between the shoulder blades. She freezes. I brace for her to spin around and unleash hell, but she doesn't. She straightens. Then, without a word, she walks out.

And that's when I hear him. The Savage.

His voice, low and electric, purring at the base of my skull. "That was just a warning shot. Don't mess with me, Bitch."

I feel his presence: coiled, dark, and potent. Something ancient and primal stirs within me.

I can sense his sinister force pulsating deep within me as I drift off to sleep.

The next morning, I wake in a dazed, throbbing state. My dream still clings to me, sticky and vivid as the images play out on my ceiling in the stillness of the dawn. I am chasing a girl from my class. We start on the playground and wind up in the woods. She runs. I hunt. Her fear is tangible, delicious and it's drawing me in deeper. I find her curled beside a fallen tree, trembling. I reach for her throat. And in that moment ecstasy washes over me.

I wake up soaked in it. Aroused. Buzzing.

As the sun begins to peek through the curtain slats, I drag myself to the bathroom. Steam fills the air as I shower, but I can't shake the dream's grip. When I step out, I wipe at the mirror trying to clear the fog.

That's when I see The Savage. Standing in the reflection behind me. Or maybe he is me. My face, but twisted. Bigger. Sharper. Stronger. My eyes are gone, replaced by black holes.

I lean closer. He doesn't mimic me. He stares back, independent. Smirking.

"Who are you?" I whisper. He grins wider, teeth gleaming.

"I am the force that gives you power. I'm your ticking time bomb who will help you settle the score. I am the hunter who will prey upon your enemies. Together we will conquer whatever we desire with no repercussions. I am the animal to your human. With me there is no room for repentance, only gratification."

Nine: Toby

I REMEMBER in middle school I learned self-regulation because The Savage consistently challenged my superiority. Controlling him was like standing in a war zone. The Savage's behavior placed us at risk for exposure. I couldn't let anyone else know about the darkness I concealed. If they saw even a glimmer of The Savage, I'd be done. Friends would evaporate. Teachers would single me out. Parents would whisper about me behind closed doors. And The Savage? He'd be exposed. I couldn't let that happen. Not yet.

Confusion constantly tore at me because most of the time The Savage's ideas made sense. I played tug of war between what The Savage wanted to say or do and what others viewed as acceptable behavior. I didn't want my friends to see me as a weirdo, so I stuck to societal rules. He didn't care about consequences, but I did. I had to.

There had been a few bouts of trouble where The Savage had completely taken over and I had lost control. These events led to a particular younger female cousin of mine tattling about what my mom and aunt called "inappropriate" behavior towards her. That word—it echoed in my ears for days. Inappropriate? Like I was too dumb to know what they were talking about.

The Savage and I decided I needed a fresh start, so we came up with the idea of changing my name to Toby, which is my middle name. Toby didn't have a reputation. Toby didn't have baggage. Toby was already popular and quite the ladies' man.

To my shock, my parents actually agreed to this brilliant idea. All summer, before school started, I think my parents used my "new name" a hundred times a day so I could get used to hearing it. By the time I started eighth grade, I hardly remembered my name had ever been Jeb. At first, my classmates and friends had a lot of questions, but eventually they also accepted my name as Toby. I think we were all so young, we just assumed this was a normal occurrence. To me, reinvention felt logical.

But even as Toby, The Savage didn't go away. He grew quieter, but I knew he was watching. Waiting.

One day our class was on the playground after lunch. A group of us sat on the sidewalk chewing the fat and complaining about the science project we were assigned earlier in the day.

Quietly my classmate Carson Ann, who was sitting next to me, pulled a baggie from her coat pocket and gestured for me to take one of her cookies. The intensity of her eyes ambushed me as she sneakily passed the homemade treat to me. It felt like a dare or a promise.

Noticing just two cookies in the baggie I discreetly extracted one for myself. My fingertips brushed against the palm of her hand through the plastic. How the heat between us did not melt the baggie was beyond comprehension.

A thick leather band with Paul's name stamped in yellow encircled her wrist. I pondered if Paul was aware his girlfriend was hot for me. The Savage did. He whispered, 'She's yours. She just doesn't know it yet.'

After school, I waited in the courtyard to escort Carson Ann to her bus. My heart thumped loudly as sweat beaded under my nose and on the back of my neck. The anticipation was killing me.

Out of the corner of my eye, I catch she and Paul holding hands as he walked her to her bus. How could she reject me? My jaw locked as I heard The Savage snarl "She's playing you for a fool."

On the bus ride home, my mind spun as I obsessed over Carson Ann's aloofness. Undoubtedly, Carson Ann tried to break up with Paul; how did he talk her into staying? Maybe Frannie, Carson Ann's loud-mouthed best friend, convinced her Paul was the better pick. The class president. The safe bet.

Every roadblock keeping Carson Ann from her true feelings for me made my blood boil.

Suddenly, I became aware a kid named Charlie sat next to me without my noticing. Taking advantage of his proximity and planting a knuckle sandwich into his bicep, I nearly knocked him off the bench seat. The look on Charlie's face told me he was not expecting the blow. My maniacal cackle commingled with Charlie's awkward laughter. Inner alarms were clanging against my skull. Recognizing my risky behavior, I warned myself to reel in The Savage before making a scene and possibly getting kicked off the bus.

Walking up my driveway from the bus stop, my anger over Carson Ann's being a tease returned in a flash. While making my afternoon snack, The Savage narrated revenge fantasies on a loop. We imagined Carson Ann alone in an empty school. Frozen in place with fear. Her stench floated through the classrooms like perfume, taunting me to find her. Her whimpers echoed through the intercom system as she hid from me.

Tracking her, I plotted what I would do to her once I finally captured my prey. My hands twitched as I pretended to restrain and choke her until her eyes popped from her skull. Power surged through my veins like electric wildfire.

Impulsively, I grabbed the kitchen phone and shakily dialed the first number on the phone list taped to the wall.

One ring... no answer. Two rings... no answer.

Third ring..."Hello." So sweet and harmless. Weak. Perfectly weak.

The voice was Ms. Edna from my mom's bridge group. This should be fun! In a low, quiet voice, I became the predator. I recounted to Ms. Edna how I was going to hunt her like a baby deer pursued by a hungry wolf through the desolate woods near her house. The description of my stroking her fear unfolded from my mind into the receiver.

Click.

The bitch disconnected before I could get to the good parts of how I would tear her body into shreds after I ravaged her. A deep, euphoric belly laugh escaped my throat as I turned on The Andy Griffith

Show and plopped onto the couch to enjoy my afternoon snack.

The interaction with Ms. Edna put me in a great mood for the rest of the night.

During the following few weeks, I anticipated Carson Ann would dump Paul enabling us to go steady. To my dismay, they never broke up. That stung. Still does.

Whenever the anger comes back as it always does, I go to the kitchen wall phone. I never call the same number twice. Just enough to scratch the itch. Just enough to keep The Savage fed.

I am careful not to ever call the same number twice since The Savage is easily bored.

Ten: Olive

O N MY DRIVE home from the pool through the country roads, I am lost in my memories. As I contemplate the two Tobies I've encountered, something tugs at the back of my brain. Toby isn't the brunt of all the school jokes like he assumes; for an average guy he's moderately popular in our school.

We are part of The Class of 1983 at The Academy. Ours will be the largest number of graduates in one class in the history of the school. We are a mighty band of 42 students, all great friends. We learn together, study together, and laugh together. Compiled of jocks, nerds, metalheads, cheerleaders, wallflowers, and scholars, we somehow gel together. As we climb the ranks of the student body hierarchy, we blaze a path of our own, leaving uniquely indelible marks in our wake.

The Academy teachers resemble extended family, most of them either parents of our friends or friends of our parents. A teacher being included on a multi-family vacation trip is not abnormal for us. Many of them had been born and raised in our hometown and had returned after college to specifically teach at the Academy. Most were alumni.

The class of 1983 is full of class clowns, individually and in groups. Because of our familiarity with the teachers, we tend to include them in our harmless antics. Ms. Spigo, one of our favorites, is an elderly spinster who lives in one of the small towns in the county. She is a brilliant chemist, but a bit gullible and unconventional. She teaches Chemistry in the only science lab on campus, where a telephone was installed in her classroom in case of a fire.

In an effort to delay class, I, being her favorite, sometimes walk to the phone and answer as if it just rang. I talk for a bit as the other students settle into their seats. I urgently tell Ms. Spigot the mayor or the headmaster or the fire chief or whomever I can conjure, is on the phone. The fake phone call habitually launches Ms. Spigot into reminiscing about her connection to the caller. Although we pull this prank on her at least once a week, she consistently and honestly falls for the shenanigans every time. The disruption delays the lesson and gets Ms. Spigot discombobulated. Class doesn't commence before the dismissal bell rings and we giggle our way to our next class.

My favorite prank we ever pulled started with Ms. Spigot getting tangled in her own feet and taking an unfortunate tumble in class one day. She forcefully crashed to the floor. We realized she was injured and needed help. None of us laughed at that point because we dearly loved the cooky woman. One student ran to get help from the office and let them know what happened while another student called the ambulance.

Craig is a volunteer for the rescue squad and surmised she would need medical treatment at the hospital. Attempting to keep Ms. Spigot laying still on the floor, a handful of us girls squatted beside her and talked to her, making her laugh in order to distract her from the pain and embarrassment of her fall. As she lay there like a brave soldier listening to our nervous babble, Toby formulated a hysterical idea. He grabbed the chalk from the chalkboard tray and outlined Ms. Spigot's body as if to make a crime scene. He convinced our sweet teacher a chalk outline would help the Headmaster and Fire Chief know the exact spot of her landing in case there needed to be an investigation. Toby nailed the prank with precision.

Once the ambulance took her away, Toby darkened

Ms. Spigot's outline approximately five more times to ensure visibility. For the remainder of the day, a parade of students filed into the science lab peeking at the crime scene. We dedicated a full page in the yearbook to Ms. Spigot, including the body outline on the classroom floor.

Our mischief generates a tight bond amongst my classmates, including Toby. His perception of being an ostracized outsider doesn't fit the narrative of his inclusion within the dynamics of our class. Typically, he is an average guy who ranks in the middle of the pack. While he isn't a leader, he isn't completely introverted either. He interacts in a normal, inconspicuous way. He doesn't date, however neither does much of the class. We socialize in big groups and couple up for the sake of attending semi-formal dances.

Preferring small groups or being alone, Toby doesn't participate in all the school activities. He skips the semi- formal dances, always assuming no girl will accompany him if asked. I don't know if this is the case, but he rarely tries to find a date and doesn't seem bothered by his lack of courtship.

As for sports, football and baseball are his primary athletics. Toby is kind of puny, so he isn't perceived as a football star. Baseball is where he excels. He made the varsity baseball team our ninth-grade year. Being in sports gives Toby a place to feel included. He gravitates toward the jocks when socializing. I wouldn't say he's popular, but Toby is accepted and never appears to be in competition to be the golden-boy amongst his buddies. He seems to appreciate being part of the crowd but a little invisible. The times Toby is the least invisible are those where his temper is on display.

I overheard rumors concerning Toby throwing his helmet or using it as a weapon, threatening a few of the younger players. The most severe claim I am aware of regarding Toby's odd behavior is how he gets off on going after the younger guys. Weirdly, he begins practice quiet and subdued but gets more rageful as practice proceeds. As his teammates tire from their physical exertion, Toby becomes more energized. Nicknamed the Dirt Devil, his eyes practically glow red from rage as practice ends. The rage follows him into the locker room where he gets amplified and hyper.

The guys tell us Toby makes bizarre sexual remarks making them feel rattled. They refuse to tell us the exact words he uses, but they say his sex rants make them uncomfortable. Usually when he starts, they grab their stuff and get away from him as soon as possible. I don't like to imagine my friends in such a state. The reality is at practice you get Dirt Devil Toby or quiet, withdrawn Toby and nothing in between. He gives the impression of existing in these two extremes.

I snap out of my focus on Toby, rounding the last curve before my driveway and pull a bit past the pavement allowing me to back my car into my designated spot. I am reversing when my mom runs screaming into the middle of the yard. She urges me to hurry as I hand-crank my window closed. She yells my name loud enough for the neighbors two miles away to hear her.

Exiting my car and shutting my door, I jog to Mom to see what is causing her to act like a psycho. Breathlessly she squeals at me and the shock of what she says makes me stumble. I think I might faint as I watch my mom's mouth move, but her words sound fuzzy.

"Toby...Olive! Toby..."

I use all my might to hear the sentence she is repeating at me. I dart into the house and crash to the floor along the hallway wall as mom bursts through the door. Kneeling in front of me, mom shrieks, "Toby killed her! Toby killed her!"

For the life of me I try to figure out who Toby might have killed. Was it a person or an animal? How could Toby have killed anything? I saw him on the bus less than two hours ago.

Eleven: Georgia

WITH THE FAMILIAR WHOOSH, I am transported to the back yard of my childhood home on the night before my wedding.

Momma's lavender always bloomed brightest this time of year. The plants flank the back steps like floral sentries, releasing a sweet, woody scent that clings to the air like a memory. One deep breath is enough to loosen every knot inside me. Lavendar has always been nature's lullaby to me.

I can remember as a small girl, I loved to tiptoe through the clumps of lavender and lightly brush the stems through my bare toes, creating a cloud of calm and tranquility. This must be what cats feel as they roll on catnip.

Painstakingly picking the finest stalks, Momma and

I took sprigs of the green and purple plant to the florist yesterday for my wedding bouquet. I remember how she hummed while she worked, her fingers moving like magic through the flowers. On the way home we stopped at three different drugstores before we finally found the perfect lavender nail polish to match the bridesmaid's dresses. I teased that we were on a mission from God, and Momma didn't even argue.

I couldn't wait to see the color on Momma against her royal-blue suit. I wanted her to feel radiant and proud.

Tonight is the night before my wedding, and we're sitting at the kitchen table. Hands resting on the wood as I gently paint her nails. My stomach is a grumbling storm, because all I concentrate on is Momma's chocolate cake. I swore off the cake for months to make sure I'm able to fit into my wedding dress, but now after all this time without my favorite treat, I am having a hard time controlling my urge. That cake calls to me like a siren! Momma jokingly announces it'll be a long time before I get cake again because I need to stay slim for my new husband. Her joking tone wraps around me like an old quilt as I feel the weight of separation looming. A new chapter is starting, but I'm grieving the old chapter closing.

I wanted momma's cake to be our wedding cake,

but she wouldn't hear of the suggestion. She wants a proper tiered cake fit for a proper bride and groom. Personally, I can't imagine anything more proper than the chocolate heaven from her oven. She probably doesn't believe her oven can handle the amount of cake needed to satisfy a hungry reception crowd. I know her cake would be the star of the entire day and night!

I can't fathom this is the last night I'll spend in this house in the company of my parents. I'll be a mere eleven miles away but the distance feels like I'll be living in a different world. Apart from college I haven't lived anywhere but in this house.

Momma catches onto my wedding jitters and anxiety about moving because later in the night she lays in bed beside me. It reminds me of the nights she would comfort me during thunderstorms, lying next to me in brave silence. Fresh from the shower, she smells of lavender soap and her favorite Jean Nate` after bath splash. I press my face into her shoulder and drink in the scent of her.

WHOOSH

Suddenly I see myself standing outside the church, my arm hooked through the crook my dad's. My flower girls and bridesmaids are floating down the aisle ahead of us in a whispering stream of lavender. The groomsmen flank Mack at the front, all standing sentry in their navy suits. I've never experienced such joy. Everything is perfect and I am loving every second of this time. I see the back of myself and Dad as we proceed to the front of the church. A cloud of lavender scent follows my image as I walk toward the altar, smiling at my loved ones as I pass. I catch the glimmer in Mack's amber eyes as he anticipates seeing his bride for the first time. He exudes pride and my heart's bursting. I long to run and take my place at the center of the ceremony, to integrate my ghostly self, but my feet won't move.

My heart is filled with warmth and nostalgia at the sight of the chapel decorated with an abundance of lavender flowers, the walls adorned with white lace and delicate strands of ivy.

The pews are wrapped in lavender satin ribbons, creating a soft, romantic atmosphere perfect for our special day. The ribbons and the lavender chiffon bridesmaid dresses are a perfect match. The girls' hair is styled in loose curls, adorned with lavender sprigs that match the bouquets they carry. The groomsmen, on the other hand, sport navy suits with lavender ties, a perfect complement to the color scheme.

As I look out over the fields that surround the chapel, I can't help but beam at the moment the church doors open, and I catch my first glimpse of my dashing groom. He looks so handsome in his navy suit, his eyes filled with love and adoration as he waits for me at the altar. He fought me tooth and nail to wear navy instead of grey or black, insisting he not be dressed for a funeral. He jokingly expressed a leading lady (that's me) needs a leading man to be debonaire and sexy, not gloomy. Mack and Momma tussled a bit because she wanted to wear navy, but we finally convinced her that royal blue or ice blue would be a great complement to everyone's attire. She only agreed once I promised we would match her nail polish to the lavender so she could feel she was supporting both sides of the aisle.

But what truly steals the show that day is Mack's labrador, Atticus, proudly carrying our rings down the aisle in a small lavender pouch tied around his neck. The guests erupt in laughter and applause as Atticus prances to the altar, wagging his tail in excitement. Atticus stops at the end of each pew, offering every person on the aisle an opportunity to pet him. As the ceremony begins, Mack and I exchange our vows, promising to love and cherish each other for all eternity.

I vow to always support and encourage Mack to be the best he could be without overworking himself, to be his rock in times of need and his light in times of darkness. Mack vows to always protect and care for me, to be my shelter in the storm and my safe haven in times of trouble. He vows to let me win at Uno once a month as long as I continue to let him be the master of the grill. And as we exchange rings and seal our vows with a kiss, I know in my heart our love will last a lifetime. As the preacher presents us as Mr. and Mrs. Bentley, we both cry with elation as do his parents and mine. At that moment, I feel the chapel's wall will burst, unable to contain all the love surrounding us.

The reception that follows the chapel wedding is held in a charming barn on Mack's family's farm. The rustic wooden beams are adorned with twinkling lights and ivy garlands, creating a warm and inviting atmosphere for the celebration. As we make our grand entrance, the guests erupt in applause and cheers, showering us with catcalls and rebel yells.

Mack and I share our first dance to "This Will Be (An Everlasting Love)" by Natalie Cole under the soft glow of lanterns, our eyes locked on each other as we sway to the music. The world blurs away as we dance, our bodies close, our souls closer. Everything else fades. It's just him, me, and the feeling of home.

Afterwards, the bridal party joins us on the dance floor for a group toast to our unending friendships. Dressed in their lavender and navy attire the group dances and laughs the night away. Merriment and delight fill the air, creating a blend of unity and happiness, enveloping everyone in attendance.

During dinner, we share a special moment as we stand at the head table, looking out over our friends and family who came to celebrate our love. We raise our glasses in a toast, thanking everyone for their support and love throughout our journey together.

As the evening draws to a close, Mack steals me away for a quiet moment alone under the starlit sky. We walk hand in hand through the fields surrounding the barn, the sound of crickets chirping in the distance as we reflect on our perfect day. Atticus trotting beside us through the open field, stars above winking like they know our secret. In that moment, surrounded by the beauty of the night and the love of each other, I know without a shred of doubt we are truly meant to be together forever.

Our future in that instant is filled with endless possibilities and unwavering love. The devotion and adoration we have always felt for each other shine brightly in our eyes. There's a hint of nostalgia and reflection in the evening as we relive all the moments that brought us to this day. Each dance step seems to carry the weight of our journey, the struggles and triumphs, the laughter and tears, all woven into the fabric of our celebration. We are grateful for the steadfast love we found in each other, for the unshakable support of our friends and family, and for the opportunity to share this beautiful moment. Overall, the reception is a perfect blend of love, joy, nostalgia, and gratitude, encapsulating the essence of our entire relationship and the depth of our connection. It is an event that touches the hearts of all who attend, a reminder of the power of love and the beauty of finding your soulmate.

If I knew my life would end in a flash, I would slow down time and stay more present. I am desperate to remain in this moment forever. I would memorize each second, find a way to suspend time.

Twelve: Toby

THIS HAS BEEN A SHIT WEEK. My mom is up my ass about my grades; coach is bugging me to attend a spring baseball clinic and now this asshole librarian is ragging on me for looking at tits in the National Geographic. My buddies and I were laughing, just being dumb, and here comes Mrs. Bernstein. The queen cow herself is marching over like she's the morality police.

She performs loud enough for everyone to hear. I guess she's never seen teenage boys laugh before. Then, in her biggest power move yet, she kicks us out of the library. "Back to class," she barks, reveling in her little moment of humiliation.

Walking back, I catch my reflection in the classroom window. My face flushed, jaw clenched. The red in my cheeks matches the heat pounding behind my eyes. I hear snickering from the back row. The girls laughing and whispering. It only confirms what I already feel: I've been made a fool. And all I can think about is payback.

After baseball clinic, I climb into Brett's truck with Beau and Chase. I chuck my gear bag into the bed and slam the tailgate. No one says it out loud, but they know I'm still stewing.

We head down to Homer's Gas & Grill. Homer's the kind of guy who's been serving underage locals since forever, no questions asked. We load a case of beer into the cooler, and the tension in my chest starts to loosen with every cold one I knock back. That familiar buzz starts crawling under my skin.

Conversation turns to her. Bernstein. Chase mocks her voice. Beau makes some lame cow impression. The more they joke, the more I fuel up. I let the words spill out: "She needs to be taught a lesson."

They think I'm kidding. But I'm not. At first, they're laughing until I unzip the hidden compartment in my baseball bag and pull out The Annihilator. It's a beautiful, brutal thing: a black-handled machete my dad picked up for me at a gun show when I turned twelve. Most kids got bikes. I got steel.

Their laughter dims. There's a flicker of unease in Beau's eyes. Good.

Black Sabbath's "War Pigs" shakes the truck's speakers as we peel out onto the county road. The music is a war cry. My heartbeat syncs to the drums. We keep the volume high until we cross the city limits, then Brett dials it down and makes a few turns. We end up parked on a side street. Where it's quiet and dark.

The Bernsteins are at the high school basketball game. We made sure.

Brett kills the engine. The silence is thick.

"So, what now, Big Shot?" Chase asks, half-joking.

I respond with a howl, "Time to have some fun!" Jumping out of truck with the Annihilator in hand I tell the boys to wait and watch. A glimmer of the metal glints in the streetlight as I unsheathe and raise the machete above my head and snarl to myself, "Time to even the score."

Their laughter follows me as I march across the front lawn. The Savage rises in me like a tide. I let him take the wheel. His rage is laced with joy. My body moves, but he's the one steering.

I swing.

And swing.

And swing.

Bushes, flower beds, shrubs—obliterated. Grass

rips beneath my feet. Wood cracks. Leaves scatter like shredded paper. The three dogwoods? Personal. Each one gets special treatment. I tear them down limb by limb, slashing until nothing stands upright. I feel untouchable. Unstoppable.

When it's over, I jog back to the truck, breathing hard and grinning like a lunatic. I wipe the blade on my pants. My friends are staring with mouths open, eyes wide.

They look shocked.

But beneath that? Awe.

They know what I am now.

We blast Led Zeppelin's "Kashmir" and tear off into the night, tires screaming, music blaring, adrenaline roaring in my ears.

The next morning, I wake still filled with the rush of having achieved total annihilation and punishment for Mrs. Bernstein's transgressions. I wonder if she cried. If she screamed. If her perfect little world tilted just enough to remind her she's not untouchable. Let's see who kicks me out of the library now.

I move through the kitchen in a daze, slowly chewing bacon and eggs while visions of the Bernsteins discovering the carnage play like a highlight reel in my mind.

Thirteen: Toby

I WANT to ask Ester to the prom, but I haven't decided how to pose the question yet. Even though I've known her since third grade, I can't get a read on her. I sure as hell don't want her to embarrass me by saying no. I'm not going to be the laughingstock of my class. All I can do is present the appealing sides of me. I've opted to help build the prom murals after baseball practice so I can put my best foot forward in front of Ester. So, I've been showing up. Being visible. Presenting the version of myself I think she might say yes to. It's not about the paint. It's about the image.

Ester still has her baby face but was the first girl in our class to get boobs. She is not overly confident but she's popular. Luckily for me, Ester is single and as far as I know, has never had a steady boyfriend. Her cute looks will make me look good to my buddies and her inexperience will hopefully enable me to score on prom night. Ester is a sure thing.

At The Academy, the Junior class traditionally decorates the gym for the Senior class prom, and we pull out all the stops. By the time we finish building the walls and decorating every nook and cranny of the gym, the Seniors will feel like they're walking into a Polynesian Paradise. We use an old farm warehouse to build and paint the murals. It smells like moldy peanuts and paint fumes, but it gets the job done. We work like dogs to finish.

I wrap up baseball, hit the showers, and head over. The song 'Fly Like an Eagle' spills out of the building, vibrating through the floorboards. I move toward my crew, trying to keep things light. I need to seem normal, even if my stomach is a clenched fist.

The heavy air is musty and smells of tempera paint. I make a bee line for my buddies. We are joking and having a good time when Susan pops by, clip board in hand, assigning duties. She designates me and Jon to fetch the mural paper from the storage shed and commence painting. We don't need drop cloths. No one cares if the old warehouse floors get smeared.

After we arrange the paper, everyone grabs brushes and bottles of paint and gets cracking. I spy Ester in the back corner working on a volcano mural and decide to join her. "It's time to make my move," I whisper to myself. I'm going to drop hints while we paint.

We greet each other and I get to work helping her. Ester says something funny. I lift my head and laugh. That's when it all unravels. Frannie comes into focus across the room. She's squatting near the mural in progress and reaching to paint the top of the paper. Every time she reaches across, I notice her cleavage and the top of her hot pink lace bra. She acts like she doesn't know she's teasing me, but that smug tilt of her head says it all.

She's trying to distract me. I can't talk to Ester while that bitch is putting on such a show. Heat rises in my chest. I need to walk away and get fresh air. I rush outside to cool off and regroup.

Outside, all I can think about is how much I hate Frannie. We have known each other since I started at The Academy. She is always loudly boasting about how she is one of the originals in our class, having started in pre-K. Frannie is a bossy know-it-all blabbermouth in a hot body. As soon as she got her boobs, she started flaunting them in everyone's face. I'll take care of that slut in due time but for now I need to focus on Ester.

Calmly, I turn and traipse into the warehouse. Gail has taken my place alongside Ester. Damn. Fucking

Frannie blew my chance to ask Ester to prom. Now, it's imperative I devise a new plan on how to hint about our potential date. The music shifts to Lynyrd Skynyrd's "Sweet Home Alabama." Everybody breaks into song. Olive and Hannah are using their paint brushes as microphones. Nick and Jim whip out their air guitars and now the whole building is rocking.

The night is ending, and we are cleaning the warehouse. I make myself look busy but I'm watching Ester, waiting for her to walk toward the door.

She grabs her keys from her purse and heads for the exit. In an attempt to escort her to her car, I quietly follow. She looks like a fairy bathed in moonlight.

I open the door to her car for her; the dash light glows on her face. She's exquisite. I warn her to be safe as I lean in for a kiss.

"Toby, wait up. Don't forget you're giving me a ride home."

Hells bells! Thanks to Olive, the moment is fucked and another opportunity has been missed.

Jerking my head, I acknowledge Olive. When I pivot back toward Ester, all I see are brake lights fading into the night. I guess I'll come back tomorrow night and try again.

Securing the materials and turning off the lights, the rest of my classmates depart the warehouse for the night. A parade of brake lights and dust clouds emanate the field as loud music and honking horns disrupt the stillness of the streets.

Olive hops in and I crank the car. I'm pissed beyond measure but I don't want Olive to know. I try to drown the thumping anger throbbing in my head as I ponder my missed opportunities. I pop in my Queen tape and blast the volume as Olive chats away. I don't know what she's saying. I just laugh when she laughs trusting she won't perceive my rage.

That night, I lay in bed, rewinding the moment. I can't stop obsessing over Frannie and the way her t-shirt kept slipping, showing me her tits. I want to rip her damn shirt off and use it to choke her. The bitch stole my opportunity to ask Ester to prom. As I am falling asleep, I grow horny with the fantasy of hurting Frannie. It settles over me like a warm blanket as I drift off.

The next day I catch wind people are going back to do more painting Friday after school so I swing by the warehouse on my way home after practice. When I don't find Ester's car, I park in the back where I can have a bird's eye view of the field without being spotted. An hour passes, and she is a no-show.

Pulling out of my hideaway, I recognize Frannie's bright green Chevy Citation taunting me exactly like

Frannie did the night before. Daring me to make a move. I wouldn't need to stalk Ester like a complete loser if not for Frannie's distracting cleavage.

Sneakily, I slink to her car, circling once then I grab onto the antennae. In one quick snap, I relieve her automobile of the appendage. If only I could linger to see the look on her face! The threat of getting caught outweighs the sight of her misery, however I take the antenna as a souvenir. "That'll teach her."

Quickly I head to Jon's house to hang. A bunch of guys are in his garage shooting pool as I arrive. The main topic of conversation is who will be asking whom to prom.

I dare not let them know my plan. I am happy no one mentions Ester's name on their list of potential dates. Maybe this means there is a good chance of her saying yes. The gathering splits by 9:00PM.

Once I'm home, Mom asks if I went after school to help paint for the prom. I lie and tell her I did. Why is she always butting into my business?

She attempts to converse, but I am not in the mood. Pretending to be hungry, I request a sandwich since I missed dinner. I am not actually hungry, but I like making her do dumb stuff for me to hinder any conversation she tries to have. She brings it up to my room, smiling like she's proud. I take the plate, close the door, and blast my stereo.

If she isn't careful, she might get whipped by my new antenna souvenir. I imagine the snap of the makeshift whip hitting the back of her legs to the rhythm of the music. The sound in my head merges with the beat from my speakers. Before I know it, I've drifted off to sleep.

Fourteen: Georgia

I'VE BEEN WORKING as a substitute mail carrier on a rural county route for the past four months.

It's my first real job since college, and I'm holding on tight to the hope that it turns permanent. Momma swears if I land a full-time gig with the post office, I'll be set for life. Mack, my husband, just chuckles. "Set for life... until we start having babies," he teases.

My workday starts early. By 7:00 every morning, I'm already elbow-deep in letters, bills, and bubble-wrapped boxes. Sorting, organizing, and loading everything into my old station wagon takes nearly two hours, but I've got it down to a system now.

At the distribution center, I've been getting to know Charlotte. She's been a permanent employee there for four years, which in postal time makes her a seasoned veteran. Like me, she started out as a sub, and her story gives me hope that mine might end the same way.

We've hit it off. Our conversations are easy and warm, usually revolving around our husbands, the quirks of married life, and her baby boy, Henry, who just turned eighteen months. Lately, we've been trading easy dinner recipes like currency. Last week, I smuggled a thick slice of Momma's chocolate cake in for her. I had to sneak it past Mack, who firmly believes sharing that cake is grounds for divorce.

Charlotte says she'll teach me cross-stitching so I'll have something to do when Mack and his daddy go hunting. In return, she wants to learn how to bake that legendary cake. We both laugh at the idea since I've tried three times and haven't come close to Momma's. Charlotte's been showing me the ropes around the distribution center, cluing me in on who to watch out for and who's worth buttering up. I don't know what I'd do without her.

By 9:00AM I've got everything loaded up and my old station wagon, Thirsty Thelma, is rumbling down the road. Leaving at nine helps me dodge the school buses and the lumbering farm tractors that creep down the back roads.

My first stop is always Ms. Johnston. She greets me every morning in her flowered housecoat, flanked by a gaggle of noisy chickens that follow her around like groupies. Next, I roll past Mr. Brady's porch. He's always out there, no matter the weather, raising his chipped coffee mug in salute. I suspect there's more than just coffee in that cup, but every time I ask, he just winks and grins.

Stop three is the Smiths, five miles up the road. I walk their mail to the door because neither of them leaves the house anymore since they both rely on walkers. I wedge the envelopes carefully behind their screen door and give it a gentle knock, just in case they're up.

Then there's Mrs. Applesmith. Lord help me, she's addicted to catalogue shopping. I deliver five or six boxes a day to her porch. Unloading all her packages is enough to throw my back out. I've come to dread her driveway, but Charlotte let me in on a juicy secret: Mrs. Applesmith gives out amazing Christmas gifts to her mail carrier. That tiny bit of hope keeps me going every time I wrestle a mountain of boxes from the back of the station wagon.

I'm learning the rhythm of the route and starting to recognize each face and its peculiar charm.

Midday, I pull into Strickland's Market. I drop off their mail, grab a Sundrop from the cooler, and pick one of their homemade sandwiches such as bologna, chicken salad, or ham, all pressed into white bread and wrapped tightly in plastic. They're all so good I've stopped trying to choose a favorite. Mr. Strickland knocks a few cents off my gas cost as a perk for being his mail lady. That discount matters when you're driving something as thirsty as Thelma.

After Strickland's, I swing by the bowling alley and hardware store, the most commercial stretch on my route. Most stops are miles apart, so this cluster is a rare moment of convenience and a chance to stretch my legs.

There's something peaceful about driving these country roads. I get to see cows lounging under trees and sheep nibbling at grass while I work. The scent of fresh-turned dirt lingers in the air from nearby fields. Sometimes, I have to stop for a herd of cows meandering across the road.

One of my favorite interruptions is Rosco, the Martins' hound. He's a known escape artist, always wriggling out and trotting over to the Wiggins' place to curl up next to their cat. He's warmed up to me now, and when I spot him on the way to deliver the Martins' mail, I scoop him up and drop him home. Technically, passengers aren't allowed, but I doubt the rules apply to hound dogs in love.

There's just one house on my route that unsettles

me. It's the last stop of the day, perched near the end of the paved road where it fades into trees. A boy lives there. He's lean and wiry, maybe fourteen or seventeen, it's hard to say. I don't see him every day, but when I do, something about him puts me on edge.

Sometimes he's just standing at the threshold of the woods, watching me. Not waving. Not smiling. Just watching.

His eyes are what get me because they're flat, unreadable and too old for his face. There's a heavy stillness about him, like he's rooted to the ground by something you can't see. He never speaks. If I knock on their front door, he doesn't answer when he is inside. Yet I always feel him watching from behind the curtains or the trees.

I wave anyway, forcing a smile, pretending I'm not bothered. He never waves back. But every time I drive away, my skin crawls, and I can't help but press a little harder on the gas.

Fifteen: Toby

SUNDAY BRINGS A NEW PLAN. A chance to reset. Recalibrate.

I drive to the warehouse to continue construction on the murals. A legion of classmates is already there working and the place is buzzing with teenage energy--jovial and light. I pull beside Frannie's car and chuckle at the sight of a coat hanger sticking up from the antenna hole. I stroll into the warehouse, go directly to Frannie, and ask what happened to her antenna.

She is trying to act all innocent theorizing someone broke the aerial off her car, but she can't fathom who would do such a thing and why. How could she not put two and two together and deduce her actions toward me last week are the direct cause? I want to scream in her face she'd be smart to watch her step, but she doesn't get it. Doesn't see the consequences trailing behind her every flirty grin.

Suddenly, someone sneaks behind me and covers my eyes. "Guess Who?" a high-pitched voice asks.

Without thinking, I instinctively grab the unfamiliar hands and jerk them forward, trying to knock my attacker off balance. I hear the person's knuckles crack followed by an unfamiliar squeal. I let go and spin to see Hannah with shock etched into her face. A handful of girls are gawking at me. What a close call! I nearly lost control and let The Savage surface in front of everyone. Embarrassed to my core, I mumble an apology to Hannah, but she already bolted across the room. Pivoting, I scan the room for Ester.

I locate her among a group building a wall of fake tropical flowers out of particle board and chicken wire. I position myself across from her and the group and pretend to help a couple guys assemble a small bridge. I can't stop staring at Ester. I refuse to look away and lose focus like last time. Plus, I need to watch for an opportunity to talk to her alone. As far as I am concerned, there is no one else in the warehouse but me and Ester. I don't ascertain the bridge is finished until Jon walks across for an assessment because I'm concentrating on Ester.

Breaking my focus, Susan shouts, "Everyone gather

while we go through our checklist and see what's left to do this week."

Following the crowd, I stride to the opposite side of the warehouse. From where I stand, I can keep Ester in my sight. Although she is sweeping, I watch her graceful strokes of the broom and envision her waltzing on the wooden planked floors. Her legs glide gracefully and I imagine her dancing across the floor towards me.

My chance is finally here. My window. My last shot.

The crowd breaks and heads toward the doors. Gathering my nerve, I missile straight to Ester who has finished sweeping. Snatching the broom, I accidentally startle her. Clumsily, I offer to put the broom away for her. She takes a step back as I fix my laser focus on her and blurt, "Will you go to prom with me?"

The words hit the air too hard. I hear them echo, loud and desperate. Static floods my head. My ears ring. Time slows to a stop.

Did I over-sell by yelling? I can't blink until she answers. The static in my ears is deafening. I barely hear her as she hurriedly replies, "Thank you, Toby, but I was already asked." She dashes away before I can respond, leaving me standing there holding the fucking broom like a fucking asshole. She departs with a group of her friends.

Just like that, it's over. I'm rooted to the spot where

Ester abandoned me when Susan shuts off the lights. Yelling for her to wait until the broom is put away, I sprint into the utility closet. Covertly, I clear a shelf of paint by swinging the handle of the broom like a bat. Cans clatter to the floor, colorful paint spattering in violent arcs. The chaos calms me. Paint is easier than people.

I hide the broom in the back corner and pull the door closed behind me like it's a crime scene I'm proud of. Let Susan find it tomorrow. Let her know I was here. Let her wonder what the hell happened.

I trot toward Susan who is waiting to secure the building. "I didn't notice you were here."

Well tomorrow you will notice I was here, you silly, stupid pig.

Blaring Ozzy's "Crazy Train," I barrel from the parking lot and drive to 7-11 to grab a Big Gulp for the road.

As I park, I observe Frannie and Alice inside the store and glimpse Fannie's bright green Citation. I put four parking spaces between us. I quietly creep to the back of her car and extract my pocketknife from my jeans. Slowly, I drag the knife leaving a scratch on the side from the back door to the front panel. I ought to carve a set of tits into the hood like the ones she flashed at me, using her pink lace bra to taunt and distract me from Ester. But not tonight. Tonight's about restraint. A message. A preview.

Then I vanish into the night, the knife still warm in my hand, and the smirk still unrolling across my face. It was worth sacrificing my Big Gulp to leave my mark on Frannie's car once again

Sixteen: Olive

AS I STEP into the gym, a wave of amazement washes over me. What was once a typical high school gymnasium has been transformed into something out of a dream. They're more than just prom decorations. They are comprised of a tropical escape and a Polynesian paradise brought to life. This year, I've had the honor of being part of the magic that made it happen. Yesterday, this room was filled with dull bleachers, a plain wooden floor, and the harsh glow of fluorescent lights. Tonight, it's something entirely different. Something breathtaking.

The ceiling, once an exposed expanse of industrial steel, is now draped in black dyed cheesecloth, softening the space with its dark, flowing texture. Gone are the glaring lights and the unsightly scoreboard.

Now hundreds of glimmering white fairy lights twinkle above, casting the illusion of a starry night sky, endless and filled with promise.

The walls, previously blank and boring, are now covered in intricate murals of vibrant tigers, majestic elephants, and lush tropical leaves. Each painting, full of life and color, transports you to another world. There's even a little wooden bridge arching over carefully placed mirrors, which reflect the flickering artificial tiki torches that line either side, casting playful shadows. The effect is so seamless, it feels like you're walking over a tranquil pond dotted with lily pads and lotus flowers.

Beyond the bridge, to the left, a small grass hut stands, with two towering palm trees framing the entrance. The air is filled with the sweet scent of tropical flowers. Beneath the palms, a simple white bench awaits, surrounded by palm fronds and a burst of exotic blooms, the perfect spot for photos.

On either side of the gym, just in front of the vibrant tropical walls, twelve round tables are set up, each covered in crisp white tablecloths. Purple and white orchids are scattered across the surfaces, adding a splash of color and elegance. Each table seats six, with small emerald-green booklets sitting at every place setting, mini pencils attached like a secret invitation.

The words Polynesian Paradise are embossed in silver on the covers, a gleaming promise of magic inside.

Inside the booklets, the names of the Senior class, the Junior class officers, and the six freshman waiters are carefully printed. The last two pages are left blank, encouraging classmates to write notes, sign their names, or leave fun messages, making each booklet a cherished keepsake to remember the evening by.

I take one last sweep of the room, making sure everything is in place before I head off to get ready for the big night. My excitement has been building for months, ever since my friend Fitz (short for Fitzgerald) asked me to be his date. I can hardly believe the day is finally here.

When he pulls up in his red '69 Camaro, my heart skips a beat. I'm overwhelmed by a flurry of nervous butterflies that seem to be fighting to escape my chest. As he chats casually with my dad in the foyer, I feel like I'm in a dream.

I'm wearing a dark green satin dress, its sweetheart neckline and capped sleeves creating the perfect combination of elegance and grace. My mom helped me dye a pair of satin heels to match the color of the dress, and she braided my long hair, weaving a green ribbon and sprigs of baby's breath throughout.

As I descend the stairs, Fitz catches sight of me and

his grin lights up the room. I can't help but return the smile as he looks incredibly handsome in his black tuxedo. His bow tie and cummerbund are the exact shade of green as my dress, and in his hand, he holds a plastic box containing a nosegay of white daisies and pink roses, their soft green ribbon woven through the stems. I can hardly breathe as I take it from him, and my hands shake slightly as I pin the boutonniere to his lapel.

The drive to the Academy, though only ten minutes, feels like an eternity. My mind races. Tonight feels so much bigger than any of our normal school days. Fitz and I have known each other since kindergarten, and we've spent years chatting in between classes and hanging out after school, but now things feel different. Since he asked me to prom, I've found myself noticing him in ways I never have before. He's more than just my friend; he's handsome, with a tan that highlights the hazel in his eyes, and a lean, athletic build from the baseball season. As we saunter into the gym, his hand wrapped around mine, I feel a wave of happiness wash over me. This is going to be a night to remember, I can feel it.

We reach the entrance, where the band is preparing to announce the Seniors. Students and their dates mill around the entrance, chatting excitedly as the lineup begins. Each Senior along with their date is announced as they cross the bridge into the Polynesian paradise. The Senior girls wear beautiful white dresses which is a tradition I'm eagerly anticipating for next year. The boys are all dressed in tuxedos, a mix of black, blue, and a few white, all proudly sporting boutonnieres. The girls carry nosegays or wear floral wristlets, each one more stunning than the last.

After the announcements, we settle in for a dinner of tender chicken kabobs and fragrant rice. The atmosphere is warm, laughter filling the air as plates are cleared away. Fitz and I, along with our friends, head to the bathroom to freshen up, joking and chatting as we go. As we pass by a table of Seniors, I overhear their discussion. Did I just hear them right? I try to hide the bristle in my shoulders as I catch the words "creepy guy hanging out in the parking lot." Please tell me this is not Toby! He promised me he would either put on a suit and join us inside or he would stay completely away from the gym tonight.

He did not take Ester's rejection well and has been brooding ever since. Snapping him out of his dismal disposition has been nearly impossible. I tried to convince him he could still come to Prom and enjoy the night with all of us. Afterall, he put in a ton of work to make this night happen, just like the rest of us. Having a date or not shouldn't prevent him from enjoying the outcome of our hard work. He kept saying maybe he would show up and make it a night for everyone to remember. I don't like how that sounded. And now, it seems he has brought his misery with him and is hanging out in the parking lot. Hopefully a chaperone will see him and make him leave. I am determined to enjoy my night with my handsome date and ignore Toby's actions.

As the night progresses, there is no more talk of Toby hanging out in the parking lot, so I assume he left and went home. He never came inside and from what I can tell, he never even spoke to anyone in the parking lot.

Seventeen: Georgia

JUNE NIGHTS in Virginia are my favorites--how the air softens just enough to make the world feel gentle again. Then the humidity of the day breaks and the mating dance of lighting bugs charms us. They flicker in the dusk like whispers of magic glowing softly in the trees, flirting with the stars as they dance in search of the perfect mate.

Mack built the sweetest covered patio in our back yard. The strung lights and my grandparents' old metal patio chairs set a tranquil scene. Mack stacked old barn planks on top of barrels for a makeshift dining table. The set-up is simple, but I love our secluded respite from the world. None of it matches, but every piece has an endearing story.

He and his dad fashioned a charcoal grill from an old metal beer keg. Mack is the grill master of the house; I am happy to be his sous chef. I love relaxing outdoors while the colors of the sunset envelop us and reflect on the plates of our late dinner. I mostly love watching Mack in his element—focused, relaxed, barefoot in the grass, and in charge.

Our boombox plays from the kitchen window providing our favorite tunes. Between the lightning bugs, the music, the sweet scent of summer, and watching my husband master the grill, I am on a natural high.

We enjoy entertaining friends and family on our little patio. On this particular June night, Mack's cousin, Jeff, and his wife, Sue, join us for dinner and cards. Mack's steaks are searing on the grill. I made a salad, and Sue brought a summer squash casserole. I'm serving Momma's chocolate cake for dessert.

Jeff and Mack crack open a couple of cold beers while Sue and I sip on wine spritzers. I tease Mack for his choice of music. Tonight, he chooses country although his usual preference is Southern Rock. He claims he's trying to change the atmosphere. Despite my ribbing, I find myself accompanying Dolly Parton, Willie Nelson, and Merle Haggard as they serenade us with slow songs across the dark back yard. Their voices mix with the melodious tunes and paint the night with the sounds of our emotions.

Dinner is delicious and the conversation is light. Our laughter echoes across the neighborhood as we raise our glasses in homage to Momma's chocolate cake.

After dinner, a serious game of Uno commences. Mack elects Sue to be the score keeper, declaring I cannot be trusted. Being super competitive, I challenge Mack to a side bet between the two of us. Whoever loses at Uno will clean the patio and kitchen. Mack assumes he's going to win for sure but in the last hand I crush him. We laugh as Sue and I break into our famous drunken victory dance. Mack chortles as he pulls me onto his lap and kisses me hard. Jeff and Sue giggle, taking their cue to leave.

We say our goodbyes and Mack and I settle back onto the patio loungers. This night has been perfect.

A million stars paint the sky while Willie Nelson sings "Angel Flying too Close to the Ground." And the crickets and frogs provide backup melody. Somewhere in the distance an owl screeches. Mockingly, Mack declares the distant owl is what my voice sounds like whenever I scold him. I pretend to be mad but I can't hide it very long.

In a moment's notice we're up and dancing under

the patio lights. We feel like the only two people in the world. Mack's strong arms envelop me, and I drink in the scent of his musk. Every note of music enchants me to fall deeper in love with my husband.

Mack leans in close and whispers in my ear, "I'm ready to talk babies."

I snicker, "Making one or having one?"

In his best Barry White impression he purrs, "Both, My Lady." Mack scoops me into his arms and carries me into the house laying me on our bed.

The owl screeches again and I speculate if the bird is trying to get my attention. I must have imagined it whispering my name as if to warn me of some mysterious danger lurking in the darkness. I am easily distracted by the romantic moves my husband is putting on me. The pale moonlight dances across our naked skin as we drift to sleep blissfully wrapped in each other's arms. Breath and body aligned, stitched together with our simultaneous heartbeats.

The following morning, I leave for work. Mack is cleaning the remnants of our party the night before. Seeing him shirtless, barefoot, in a pair of his work jeans, his hair wet from a recent shower, makes me want to entice him back inside into bed. Instead, I kiss him long and slow and let my hands linger on his chest, letting him know he is an exceptional housewife.

We laugh, kiss more, and off I go to undertake my day. I already miss him and long to return home for another June night on our patio. Another sanctuary beneath the stars. Another chance to hold this kind of magic in my hands and never let go.

Eighteen: Toby

JUNE 2ND GREETS ME with a sick feeling in my stomach—but not the kind from nerves, not exactly.

I'm supposed to meet Olive at the county library for a so-called "study date." It's for our Geometry exam. Two exams a day and I can barely keep track of what classroom to go to next. But Olive? She's probably been preparing all week. I've seen her flipping through flashcards on the bus, chewing on the end of her pencil like it's part of the plan.

I haven't done a bit of studying, and honestly, I don't care. This isn't about Geometry. This is about what I want.

Choosing an outfit takes longer than it should. I want to look like I didn't try, but I did. Jeans and my dad's vintage Elvis tee (a subtle flex). Her whole family worships the guy, so it's practically a guarantee. A few spritzes of Stetson, enough to make me smell like the guy she thinks I could be. The guys'll rag on me for the cologne, but they always do when I'm two steps ahead.

I see Olive on the bus, sitting midsection like she always does. I pass by her without stopping, giving her a casual nod. I'm playing the long game. Let her come to me. Let her wonder. She'll spend the whole ride imagining me, wondering why I didn't sit beside her, craving that space I've created. I can feel her desires for me multiply as the bus bumps along mile after mile. Surely the other riders must feel the electricity between us.

I'm not stupid. I know she's got feelings. She practically throws herself at me. The way she finds me at lunch, the way she always needs a ride, the way she hovers. She said yes to this "study date" without hesitation. She wants it. She just needs a little push. But there's someone else who's been circling my thoughts.

The mail carrier is probably in her late twenties. She drives her station wagon like it's part of her. Every time she uses our driveway to turn around, she waves. Sometimes she smiles. There's something hiding in her eyes. I see it. I feel it. She's into me. She just needs the right moment.

I'll create that moment.

But for now, it's about Olive.

On the bus ride home, I'll spring the plan. I'll offer to drive her to the library in my dad's car and make it feel spontaneous, like I'm just being nice. After the "studying," we'll head out somewhere more secluded. Just us. Alone. Somewhere quiet. Somewhere private.

Last weekend, I scoped out a spot: a clearing behind a cornfield, tucked away in the pine barren. It's perfect. Nobody to interrupt. Nobody to hear her if she changes her mind and needs a little coaxing. And there is no way we will be interrupted by any of her pesky friends.

Nineteen: Olive

THE MORNING of June 2nd greets me with a dull ache behind my eyes and the weight of impending exams pressing down on my chest like a wet blanket. I'm instantly stressed over my upcoming exams. I've never been a good test taker. Since no Seniors or smart people will be at today's exams, there will be hardly anyone at school to impress. I grab a balled-up tee shirt and throw on a stale pair of jeans.

I haphazardly twist my wet hair into a braid. If I could get away with it, I would toss on a ball cap as well. I catch my Pop Tarts as they jump from the toaster, burning the tips of my fingers as I leave to catch the bus.

Toby boards the bus with a rigid gait, like he is

playing the role of a soldier in an imaginary play. He can be bizarre at times. He doesn't even sit in his usual spot. Instead, he parks himself up front, tossing me a cryptic head nod that feels more like a warning than a greeting. My eyes trail him, confused.

His hair is wet and coiffed, minus his usual ball cap. Did he get dressed in his dad's closet this morning? Props to the Elvis shirt, but he will surely catch crap about his apparel from the guys. They are sure to eat him alive. It's a...statement. I just don't know what it's trying to say.

Puzzled by his appearance, I shake my head and quietly question his agenda as I crack open my English study guide to review before I get to school. Under my breath I mutter "What are you up to, Toby?" My poor brain is saturated from studying. The words on the page blur as I give in to the benefit of daydreaming. My mind wanders to all the places I would rather be than taking exams at the end of the school year as I unconsciously relax.

One of my favorite places to frequent is the country club pool accompanied by my favorite gals. Basking in the warm sun, our skin turns golden brown as we discuss anything and everything. Except for Alyssa. With her strawberry blond hair, she only burns and turns back to white. That alabaster skin just won't tan!

The pool is our summer headquarters. Everything important happens there. Secrets are traded like currency. Strategies whispered through sips of Tab and shared sunscreen. It's where we decide who's hot and who's not, which parties to hit and which boys to avoid like poison ivy. This is where the summer plans are hashed out and then reported on through the season. And we talk about hair care like it's a science, mascara like it's magic. But mostly, we talk about boys. Always the boys. Who's off-limits. Who's breaking hearts. Who might be next.

By the time the bus pulls up to school, my brain has completely checked out of test mode and firmly planted itself on a lounge chair in the sun.

As I make my way off the bus at school, Alyssa catches me, and we fall in step to our classroom. She mentions our girl group is planning to meet at the pool in the afternoon after school since tomorrow is our last day of the school year.

I hesitate for a split second, the county library flashing in my memory. Toby and I had planned to study after school. Geometry. So many theorems. So little excitement. Then I shake my head saying, "Of course I am gonna meet y'all there!" For emphasis, I flip my braid around to the side of my neck and whip it to the other side. As if studying for Geometry would ever take precedence over a poolside girl tribe meeting! Toby will survive. He always does, right?

Twenty: Georgia

JUNE 2, 1982. I AM DYING.

All those years in Sunday school and church learning the details of the afterlife, but no one ever teaches you what to do upon death. If I die, will I feel dead? What does dead even feel like?

I don't see a light or hear a voice therefore I'm not sure if I'm dead or alive. Maybe I'm in shock. How did I get here?

I remember I was in my car delivering mail and singing "More Than a Feeling" along with Boston on the radio as I approached the last stop on my route. From the corner of my vision, I saw the weird kid in the tree line. My window was open when I reached to put the mail in his mailbox. I watched a gust of wind blow a small letter out of my reach. The envelope hopped along the ground and landed at my back tire. I exited the car, grabbed the runaway, and stuck it in the box.

My door slammed as I slid into the seat. Simultaneously, my passenger door popped open. The creepy boy was suddenly beside me in the car with a hunting knife in his hand.

My eyes fell on the serrated tip. The blade looked like it was close to 8 inches long and splotched with rust, or maybe it's covered in blood.

AND NOW I can't stop staring at the knife.

The scene I'm caught in seems other worldly as if I'm in a cartoon. My mind can't reconcile the chaos. Everything is moving in slow motion.

He emits a low, guttural, animalistic growl.

I am covered in chills and the hair on my arms and neck stands at attention. A blanket of fear smothers me.

Another growl and the words, "Drive bitch."

Initially I contemplate not driving anywhere in the company of this monster. Next it dawns on me, I have no choice. I'm in the middle of nowhere at the beginning of a dirt road and there is no one close to help me. If I run, he'll catch me. If I scream, no one will hear me. My only option is to drive.

How am I going to escape?

Tears streak down my face and I shiver at the notion of what he wants from me. If I'm going to get through this, I have to give him what he wants. Crying silently, I put the car in gear and creep along the dirt path at his command.

Suddenly my survival instincts kick in. No! I'm not doing this. I'm not giving into him. I'm going to fight. I scan my surroundings trying to find a way to flee from this nightmare. There's bound to be a way out. If I drive slow enough maybe I can formulate a plan.

He yells for me to accelerate just as I spy a truck coming into view. The truck is parked on the side of the road in front of the church. Impatiently my captor pokes me with the tip of his knife and again screams at me to hurry.

I mash the gas pedal and aim for the bumper of the truck. Maybe, if I make enough noise by crashing, the owner of the truck will come help me. This is my sole shot at survival. I grip the steering wheel and close my eyes bracing for impact.

I hear metal on metal before I feel the collision. Attempting to throw my attacker off balance has failed because I don't have enough space to cause a big smash before I swerve into the truck. My assailant is not fazed by the crash and remains trained on me.

I feel bee stings along my side. Not stings! Stabs!

My attacker has begun to kill me. I throw one hand to block the knife while I reach for the door handle with the other. I pull on the handle but the blows from the knife are throwing me off balance. My hand slips. I need to escape this car. I'm blinded by fear and adrenaline. The knife is coming at me again and again. I hear a deafening train whistle in my head. Terror encompasses me like a heavy, suffocating veil.

I stop blocking the knife. I need both hands to open the door. I know if I stop blocking, he's going to plunge the knife deep into my bones, but if I stay in this car I'm surely going to die.

I move a little and manage to get both hands on the handle and pull. I hear the latch click and lean into the door. The weight of my attacker grinds into me.

We tumble from the car. He's tethered to me in some way.

Kicking and swatting at him with all my might, I attempt to escape his grip. He keeps plunging his knife into me.

I don't feel the pain anymore. I just want him off me. "Why is he doing this to me?" I think between blows. I don't know where I am anymore. I am losing the battle. I scream for Mack to come help me.

Fatigued beyond comprehension, I am exhausted from my fight to stay alive. I'm alone.

"Somebody, anybody please help me." I hear myself whimper as I beg for my life. The stench of dirt and the taste of my blood overwhelm me. On my back, I look to the anchor of the clear blue sky but all I see are dark clouds swirling.

"Mack!!!" Fighting through tears, I hear my hoarse voice call out to my husband over and over.

The sound of my heartbeat thrashes in my ears as I hyperventilate. Black spots surface in my vision as the surroundings darken. My limbs tingle with weakness. I struggle to form words with my gummy mouth.

"Mack!!!"

Can anyone hear me? Will this wretched torture ever end? Why won't he stop stabbing me?

My breath comes in slow and shallow gasps. Despair inundates my being. Anguish encases me as my throat expels a deep gurgle. One last wheeze and it is over.

MY EYES FLUTTER open as the stench of the dirt floor of our barn awakens me. I yell for Mack once more. I need him to save me. As I walk through the barn, I see Mack with his back to me. He hovers above the engine of the tractor.

I hear him singing along to the radio. Boston's "Oh What a Feeling" is blaring on the radio. He can't carry a tune but I love to hear him sing while he thinks no one is listening.

I need to get his attention so I scream using all of

my might. "Mack, stop singing. Pay attention. Help me! I'm in trouble, Mack."

I try to move closer to him but something won't let me. The more I try the further from him I get. Suddenly, Mack jerks his head around and looks directly at me. "Mack, Mack!"

He stands straight up and says, "Georgia?"

I keep screaming his name and he keeps saying, "Georgia?" He can't see me.

He turns and walks from the barn. He's looking for me. "Georgia, where are you?" He stands with his hands on hips and listens. He's as still as a statue willing his ears to find the direction of my voice.

Confused, he shrugs and walks back into the barn. "Georgia, are you in here?"

The sound of my voice is carried away by a sudden breeze. My energy is depleted. I have no more words, merely tears of resignation.

I moan, "Mack, I'm here." I can see the fine hair on his arms rise. He closes his eyes for a second and walks back to the tractor shaking his head.

I close my eyes in frustration as I surrender to the inevitable approach of my finality. I open them to find that I'm standing in Momma's kitchen.

In my peripheral, the sheriff's car backs from my driveway. Momma sits at the kitchen table and Dad stands beside her, rubbing her back. Why is Dad home from work in the middle of the day? I have never witnessed him rub her back in such a way. I call their names, but they don't respond. Momma is sobbing and Dad looks broken.

I call out to them again. "Mom, Dad what is happening? Why was the sheriff here? Who got arrested?"

Again, they don't respond. I hear my mom say "My sweet Georgia. My baby girl. She can't be gone!"

"Momma! I'm standing right here! Look at me! Can't you hear me?"

Why am I being tormented with the images of my family suffering? I must be in Hell. No way! I'm going up, not down. I know this in the root of my soul, but I expected a bright light and robed angels playing harps. I squeeze my eyes shut and Etch A Sketch my head back and forth trying to reset the scene.

Twenty-One: Toby

THE SCHOOL DAY is dragging despite being a half-day.

As I expected the guys mocked my choice of the Elvis t-shirt and cologne.

Beau joked, "The 50s called and they want their shirt back!"

Then Jon piped in and said, "Did you marinate in your dad's cologne because you reek of old men and broken dreams?"

I chuckled along, with a forced grin. Let them laugh. Let them mock. Because soon they'll be eating their words. Tomorrow, I'll be the one wearing victory like cologne. I'll hold power in my palms, and they'll beg for scraps of the story. Today I'll let them be clowns. Tomorrow I'll be the king sitting on his throne of power. That dream shatters in an instant.

As I make my way to my English class for the last exam of my day, I bump into Olive. I ignore the weird expression on her face. I continue to act nonchalantly, nevertheless I am floored by her announcement that she is ditching our study date to go hang by the country club pool in the company of her bitch friends. She tossed me aside as nonchalantly as she tosses her hair!

All of my plans crumble into dust and leave on the wind. My breath is caught in my throat as deep embarrassment crashes against my brain. I won't be bragging tomorrow. I dressed like this for nothing. Why are these bitches always ruining my plans? I hate them all enough to strangle them with my bare hands. I want to snatch Olive by her scrawny neck and squeeze until she changes her mind. But instead I pretend it doesn't matter even though inside I am a storm.

I won't be a joke in my own story! Wait 'til I get my hands on all those stupid girls, Olive's friends. They realize EXACTLY what they're doing by persuading her to cancel our plans. I'll spend my summer hunting each one of them down and making them pay.

Needless to say, my English exam kicks my ass. I need to pull a C on the exam to pass for the year and keep my parents off my butt. I'm not sure I'll make the grade since my revenge plans are a serious distraction. Thank God, the final bell rings and I get the hell out of the stifling classroom.

I board the bus and make a bee line for the back seat. I want to be alone. I am extremely pissed. Nobody should mess with me, or I'll let The Savage destroy this entire bus.

I perch myself in the middle of the seat to ensure nobody can join me. Glaring through the window I feel the heat of my anger consume me. We're halfway home before I detect Olive waving her hands at me to get my attention. What could she possibly want now? Wait, maybe she changed her mind about our date. I shoot her a disinterested head nod.

She is asking me if I'm aware of what happened between Alyssa and Earl. I tell her I know the story to get her to shut her mouth. My plan backfires when she motions me to move closer and give her the details.

I have no interest in the antics of Alyssa and Earl, but I suspect Olive wants me close to her because despite canceling our date, she's still hot for me. I move closer to appease her, believing this might be my last chance to change her mind. If I can make her laugh, then she will feel the heat of our attraction and agree to blow off her girlfriends.

Making my way up the aisle, I resolve at the last

minute to join her in the seat so I can charm her into changing her mind about canceling. I force a smile and recount the story for her, and she laughs. I continue narrating more funny stories from the day, including Beau's comments on my Elvis t-shirt. I pause in between stories, letting my charm sink into her.

When she laughs, it's a drug. As Olive cackles I notice the little kid sitting in front of us. She is turned in her seat, facing us and listening to our conversation.

I can't afford to let her distract Olive from our moment. Honestly, I want to smack the glasses right off her rosy cheeked face, but I hold back. Why is this little brat staring at me? She acts like she knows me. I see her judging me, so I demand she to stop being nosy. The brat ignores me. She has no idea who she's dealing with.

Her chin is resting on the seat in front of us and she won't stop staring at me. I growl at her to face the front. This kid is undoubtedly antagonizing me. Lucky for her she finally heeds my warning and swivels to face the front of the bus. Olive defends the brat which irritates me more.

I half hear Olive mention our English teacher, Ms. Ross. She starts laughing which makes me laugh in return, but at this point The Savage has begun to emerge. He encourages me to throw the little blonde-haired girl out the window by her throat. I fight to stay mellow on the outside guaranteeing Olive won't encounter The Savage.

I'm barely listening to Olive, when I catch the brat turned back to face us. Her beady eyes are drilling into me again. This time her hands are placed purposely in my personal space. My vision blurs with red edges, and I explode, aiming a punch toward her knuckles. Olive blocks my jab; my fist hits the seat. I envision grabbing the little imp's throat and squeezing until her eyes burst. Instead, I land another blow onto the brat's fingers. A black hood veils my sight. A cacophonous train whistle blares in my ears. I fight the urge to kill everyone left on this stupid bus.

Suddenly, we are at my bus stop. As I stand to leave, I remember Olive never re-accepted our date. I put on a show for her and she gave me nothing. How could that conniving bitch take this opportunity away from me? I calculated every move down to the last minute and now, in a flash, my conquest is stolen. As I pass Olive, I jab an elbow into her back and storm off the bus.

I'm left standing in my driveway with nowhere to put the rage coiling inside me. If I let The Savage loose, maybe I could relieve myself from this built-up wrath. One day soon he will break free.

I stomp into the kitchen and grab the phone with

the intent of placing another phone call to an unsuspecting target but I suspect that game of cat and mouse won't be enough to appease me. Not anymore. Something permanently changed inside me today. Something tells me there is no going back.

I refuse to go to school tomorrow as a virgin.

Noticing the time, I slam the phone into the cradle and head into my bedroom. Under my bed is my old hunting knife. Clipping the sheath to my belt, I tuck the weapon under my shirt. I walk outside and post myself inside the tree line of our road and await my prey. The trees embrace me with the shield of their shade.

This is it. The Moment. Finally, I'm going to let The Savage take control. So together, we wait.

We hear the music before the car appears around the curve. The mail carrier is right on time. Our senses start tingling as her scent grows closer and more intoxicating. We're going to get what we deserve. She stops her vehicle in the driveway and hops from her car to chase a piece of mail which has fallen to the ground.

We crouch low and sprint to the front passenger door. With perfect timing, we let ourselves into the car as she returns to the driver's seat. We slither as close as we can to her and unsheathe our knife, pressing the point against her cheek. We force our mouth to her ear.

The Savage snarls with a grin, "Drive, bitch."

I can feel a smile spread across The Savage's beastly face as I watch my spittle trickle down her cheek. Getting what I want is going to be quick and easy with The Savage in charge. We demand her to drive down the dirt road to the pine trees at the end.

She seems resistant, but our knife against her side convinces her to press the gas. But why is she driving this slowly? We don't want to give her enough time to formulate an escape. We scream for her to keep driving until we tell her to stop.

We're close enough to her face to taste her fear; we feel our thirst surge. We direct her again to go faster. We're immersed in her terror and don't see the truck until we crash into the bumper. This bitch blew her chance to survive.

We don't hesitate and plunge our knife into her side. Every stab releases the white-hot pressure of our rage. We slash at her body and reach to get her pants off before she has a chance to open the door. If she surrendered, we would stop stabbing her. She's using her arms to block the knife, preventing us from unbuttoning her pants. We rip her shirt apart a moment before the door swings open and we fall to the ground.

Our rage erupts. Each plunge of the knife into her flesh brings forth the memories of all the girls who wronged me throughout my life. The knife is my confession as we stab the little brat on the bus. And Olive and her bitch friends. We stab Frannie, Carson Ann, and Ester. We stab the librarian, my mother, and those two bitches who got away from me on the road. The sweet release of revenge fills our senses. We stab until my arm goes numb.

Standing over her body, we decide to land one last blow. Looking into her glazed eyes, we lift her out of the dirt and drag my knife across her neck. The opening of the flesh was in slow motion allowing me to gaze upon the curiosity of her body's reactions to my blade. Her rejection is forever silenced. As blood seeps from her wounds, I feel The Savage retreat as if he was depleted. Satiated.

I dash for the woods. I can run these woods barefoot and blindfolded. I know them like the back of my hand. The shadows of the trees create a black tunnel until my back yard comes into focus.

An unfamiliar dog barks in the distance. Realizing I have blood on my t-shirt, I rip it off and toss it onto the well cap.

Stopping in the kitchen to rinse off the knife, I wipe my bloody hands on my jeans. Calmly, I stroll to my bedroom and hide the knife in my tackle box under the bed. Taking a few deep breaths to steady my nerves, I casually walk outside and sit on the back stoop.

For the first time in years, The Savage is completely silent. I don't feel him at all. Maybe I left him beside the mail carrier or maybe he was a figment of my imagination all along. I don't have the energy to find that answer. I stiffen as I listen for what might be coming.

The dog in the distance is nearing like a dark storm moving across the sky. I close my eyes and feel my soul steeped in the release of what I have done. I am completely at peace – adrift on a euphoric high.

I hear a blood hound bark as two sheriff's deputies walk into my backyard. At first, they strike up a causal conversation, asking me if this is my house, what my name is, and what I've been doing today. Their voices are friendly and light until they spot the bloody t-shirt on the well and take note of scratches down my side.

The hand cuffs click easily around my wrists at first but tighten as I'm led away from my yard for the last time.

Twenty-Two: Olive

I STARTLE myself awake from a fitful slumber.

Bolting upright, I exclaim "He killed her! Toby killed the mail lady!"

At first, I'm in disbelief, but between the police traffic, blaring sirens, and the hushed chatter of the neighborhood adults, the reality of Toby's heinous crime is undeniable.

My friend, my ride to and from school events, my classmate, my neighbor, Toby, is a vicious murderer? How can this be? If I hadn't canceled on him yesterday, would I be his victim lying dead in the dirt? As far as I know, Toby and Georgia were not acquainted. I barely knew her through her sister, who was a vacation bible school friend.

Through overheard bits and pieces, I have compiled

a few of the details. From what I can discern, Toby attacked Georgia with a knife in her car in front of the country church. They rolled from the car as he continued to stab her, slit her throat, and eventually run to his house. He was arrested right in his backyard. But why was Toby in the mail carrier's car? Did he force his way in or was she giving him a ride somewhere? This has to be a mistake! Surely, I will get the right story once I get to school.

Wait! Am I actually required to go to school and still take my exams today?

A multitude of questions are swirling in my mind. I can't bring myself to get on the bus without Toby. After much negotiation, my mom allows me to drive myself to school. The stipulation is I cannot go alone. I phone Ester to see if she will ride with me. I pick her up a little earlier so we can compare stories with other classmates before the school day starts.

On the way, we listen to the local news radio, WLQM 101.7. We hear the newscaster report a male student from The Academy was arrested for murder, and because he was a minor, his name will not be released to the public. The reporter describes the location of the murder scene and how the Postmaster General from Virignia confirmed the victim is a young substitute mail carrier whose route included Southampton County.

Although the recounting of the story is correct, Ester and I both agree the police arrested the wrong person and they confused Toby for someone else. Once at school, we join a group of students gathered in the parking lot adjacent to the library. All the boys from our class are accounted for except one—Toby.

We don't cry or comfort each other. We vacantly stare at the ground in shocked silence. Our normally boisterous voices muted by vivid imaginary scenes playing in our minds.

The details of the homicide are horrendous, and we can't bring ourselves to discuss them aloud. Every once in a while, one of the boys alludes to the idea that they should have seen the tragedy coming. Some of them act as if we shouldn't be shocked by Toby's actions. The notion they present sends cold shivers down my spine. The icy hand of fear grips the back of my neck, and I can't stop replaying "what if" scenarios.

I'm terrified someone will mention my broken plans with Toby yesterday. Am I responsible for a woman's murder? What if I had studied with Toby at the library instead of going to the pool with the girls?

Heavy dread settles in the pit of my stomach as we

all shuffle into the classrooms to begin the last day of our Junior year. My upcoming vacation to England gives me solace to get through this terrible day. In ten days, I will escape this madness. Since my trip includes mostly underclassmen, I doubt anyone will realize I was the last student to see Toby on the day of the attack.

Before starting the Geometry exam, our teacher stands at the front of the classroom to make an announcement. She mentions the "incident" involving one of our classmates as if we don't know she is referring to Toby's arrest. She goes on to acknowledge rumors circulating throughout the school and explains this is not the time to discuss or speculate on the disturbing event but is instead the time to take our exams and close out the school year.

And with that, we take out our pencils, calculators, and scratch paper and begin our laborious exam.

I can't remember one word or symbol from the exam packet. How I got a B completely mystifies me. We obey the teacher's instruction of silence despite our desperation to ruminate on the news together.

The day ends the same way it started – with shock and horror over the accusations against our friend. The school year usually ends with a celebration; however, those plans fizzle due to the somber mood. The hushed completion of our Junior year leaves an indelible mark on our memories.

Twenty-Three: Toby

THE RIDE to jail is silent.

I stay calm, knowing eventually I'll go home to my parents. As long as I don't admit to what The Savage did, the cops cannot keep me in jail. I will never confess because I will always protect my dark companion the way he protects me. Besides, the mail carrier deserved what she got. If she surrendered to my demands, she would be alive, and we would both be at our homes by now. Technically, The Savage is the one who stabbed her, not me. And now, The Savage is seemingly dormant.

The night drags on for what seems like an eternity. First, they took my clothes and gave me a baggy jump suit to wear. They even took my shoes and socks.

Currently, a parade of detectives are attempting to

talk to me, but I cut our conversations short. I stick to my story. After school I went home, ate a snack and played with my cat which is how I got the scratches on my back and sides. Then I fell asleep.

No, I did not see the mail carrier during the day.

No, I did not leave my house after I got home from school.

Participating in the lineup is awkward because I recognize a few of the other guys standing alongside me. We are not to speak or look at each other as we enter the room and stand on a platform with height measurements painted on the wall behind us. After a 45-minute ride, I arrive at the Juvenile Detention Center sometime after midnight.

Stark fluorescent light startles me from sleep and I struggle to remember where I am. The musty, scratchy blanket is not enough to warm me from the cold metal bunk. My cell reeks of urine and body odor, sending a gag to the back of my throat. Rolling from my bed, I steady myself on the sticky floor. The filthy walls decorated with cryptic hand-scratched messages close in on me. A gruff guard passes a food tray through the slats of the metal bars. Another gag catches in my throat.

After I choke down the disgusting breakfast of cold oatmeal and lukewarm milk, I'm ushered into a visiting room where my parents await me. Exhaustion is etched on their pale faces. My dad obviously has been crying, which I've never seen before. My mom is quietly sobbing and her tears irritate me. She constantly acts like a wounded bird, always playing the victim. My dad won't make eye contact and stares at his shoes as he explains to me what to expect over the next few days.

My mom whispers in a quivering voice, "Why, Toby?"

I stick to the same story I told the detectives at the police station. I went home and fell asleep and do not remember anything else. So, there is no answer to her question.

Mom leans back as if to add space between us and mutters, "Are you sure you don't remember?"

My stomach clinches with the realization she's not buying my perfectly rehearsed story.

She has the audacity to look at me like I'm lying. She never did understand me!

The uneasy silence between us is palpable. I'm relieved as the visit ends. As I'm escorted away my dad's voice echoes, "We love you, son." My mom is still sniveling as she leans on his shoulder for support.

The first few days in juvie are a haze of cold metal, louder-than-necessary voices, and the suffocating stench of bleach trying to scrub out the rot of too many young men.

I haven't spoken to anyone since I was processed. The guards don't bother me unless it's for food, medication, or another shrink appointment. They don't have to. The silence inside me is louder than anything they could say. It clangs against the inside of my skull like a ballpeen hammer striking the inside of a bell. Even when they speak to me, it's hard to hear their voices above the roar of silence echoing through my ears.

The fluorescent lights never shut off. Not really. They hiss and flash like they're arguing with each other. I lie on the metal bunk at night, tracing the cracks in the concrete wall with my eyes, pretending I'm somewhere else without cages and guards and the acrid stench of fear, sadness, and the undercurrent of anger. This must be how The Savage feels all pent up inside me.

Sometimes I pretend I'm back in the woods around my house. From a distance, I watch Dad and Mom on the back patio, listening to Mom's songs on her boombox and laughing together. That memory is a lie I made up in my mind to keep from crumbling.

Because here's the truth: I don't miss them.

Not really.

I miss freedom. I miss choice. I miss the before. Way

before. I miss being a kid, before The Savage became so real. I miss not knowing about The Savage and how connected we became. And I miss my cat the way she would run over to me when I laid on the floor. She would curl up as close as possible and purr the loudest purr. She was never scared of me. She trusted me and I trusted her. I miss being trusted.

Every sound echoes in here. The walls are listening and recording the memories into the drywall. The clang of heavy metal doors slamming shut. The squeak of shoes against linoleum. The muffled crying that floats down the hallways at night. These are the lullabies of broken boys.

On day three, a guard who hasn't spoken to me before slides my tray through the slot and mutters, "Better eat this time. No special treatment."

I stare at the congealed mess of beige and brown on the tray. I don't touch it. Not because I'm making a point, but because my stomach lurches with trepidation. My hunger feels like the only thing I still have control over. But I know I have to eventually get used to the food because I need to keep my strength up. The Savage does not like weakness.

I haven't seen another kid up close since intake. They're keeping me separated "for safety," but I know what that means. It means I scare them. It means the guards walk slower and quieter when they pass my cell. They don't make eye contact. They don't want to get too close to The Savage.

I wish I could tell them I'm not a threat.

I wish I could believe it.

But there are moments, brief and terrible moments, when I remember flashes of red. Not the kind of red you see on shirts or apples. But the red that seeps from skin and won't stop. It's in my dreams now, lurking beneath my eyelids, splashing my thoughts like a movie reel stuck on a loop. The look in her eyes. First terror, then sadness, then nothing. The sound of her gasp. Gurgling and wet with her own blood. The warmth oozing around my fingers.

I wake up sometimes gripping the edge of the bed like it's her neck. I hear low, guttural noises seeping from my throat. Sweat beads down my back and mixes with the sour smell of my bedsheets. I strain to hear or feel The Savage with me in my memory, but The Savage hasn't spoken since that day. Not a word. I don't know if he's hiding or watching.

On the fourth night, a new kid is escorted past my cell. His wrists are cuffed, his face bruised and swollen. A tough scowl is etched into his face. He has a confidence like he's been here before. He looks at me for a second too long. I don't flinch. I make sure of it. I think I feel The Savage coil deep in my belly.

The guard shoves the kid forward and they disappear into the next block. But for a flicker of a second, I imagine The Savage standing behind me so I'm not alone—whispering in my ear, daring me to act, to reclaim some kind of power. His menacing stature towers above all and I see our shadows melded together so no one really sees me, but they see him and assume it's me. Dark and silent, commanding respect.

And I wonder if maybe I'm not alone in here after all. Maybe none of us are. I wonder how many others are concealing their own dark passenger. I wonder what would happen if all our dark passengers met and then I imagine their shadows crawling along the corridors at night when everyone is asleep. I can see them communicating with only glowing red eyes and grinning toothy mouths as they watch us in our fitful slumber.

Twenty-Four: Olive

THE HALLWAYS have never felt louder or more accusatory.

Every slam of a locker makes me flinch. Every laugh sounds sharp, almost violent, like it's been sharpened against my ribs. I keep my eyes on the ground, letting the scuffed tile blur into a single smear of gray and white.

The words float around me like smoke. Not loud. Not clear. But they cling.

"... her close friend, right? They were neighbors."

"She had to know."

"I mean, you don't just not know when someone's like that."

The hushed chatter makes me feel like I'm walking through a bad dream where everyone knows something

I don't, except this is real. They're talking about me. About Toby. About Georgia.

Georgia.

My chest squeezes so tight I almost stumble. The snippets from the radio news report flash in my head as I remember the taped-off church parking lot, the arrest of a student from The Academy. "Stabbed to death" clangs inside my brain on a constant loop.

I imagine Toby in handcuffs. His face blank like it didn't mean anything. In my mind, I see him give the same casual head nod he gave me on the bus yesterday. As if we are sharing a secret as they push him into the back of a squad car. But this is no secret I want to be a part of.

I laughed with him. I told him about my dad's gallbladder surgery while eating pizza in the courtyard. I rode home with him from ballgames, school, and even prom decorating. We listened to the radio together, singing along to our favorite songs. We shared... life.

The Toby I know wouldn't do this. But he had.

Lost in thought, I round the corner too fast and run straight into Frannie. She jumps back as if I threw a punch at her. "Sorry" I mutter, stepping sideways, trying to keep moving and putting space between us.

But Frannie doesn't move. Her eyes flick around, checking who is nearby. Then back to me. "Hey," she whispers to avoid being overheard. "You probably shouldn't be walking around by yourself."

I stare at her blankly. "What? Why?" Frannie's mouth presses into a tight line. "People are... saying stuff. That you maybe knew. Or helped him."

Her words hit me like a slap as I feel confidence breaking inside me. "But that's not true."

"I know," nodding too quickly she continues under her breath.

"I said that too. To Alyssa. And Ester. But people are scared."

I feel the burn behind my eyes. "Yeah. I'm scared too." My voice sounds rough. "We all were friends with Toby. Not just me."

Are my friends looking at me sideways like I knew this was coming?

There is a silence between us that feels jagged. Frannie shifts her weight, uncomfortable. "Did he ever... say anything to you? About stuff?"

My breath hitches. "No!" But then I ponder it. "I don't know. We talked about everything but nothing special. Just normal talking. The same way I talk to you."

Yes, sometimes Toby would seem creepy. We all thought he was just quirky. That was the worst part. That Toby hadn't seemed like someone who could do something like this. But he had. Which meant either he'd been hiding it all along... or I was too blind to see it.

At lunch, I don't sit with anyone. I spy my usual table—Alyssa, Ester, Frannie, all hunched close together behind a wall built from whispers. They don't look at me and maybe I don't want them to. So, I find a spot in the dirt under the shade of a big tree, where the leaves cast shadows like fingers reaching for me. My sandwich stays wrapped. My apple rolls out of my lunch bag into the dirt, but I don't chase it. I pick at my chips and pick at the memories in my brain. I eat my lunch alone with my thoughts. I don't feel like being with anyone right now. I especially am not strong enough to sit amongst the hushed whispers about Toby or speculation about me and Toby. I sit in silence and consider the word accomplice. Not in the legal sense. Just the way it feels to be adjacent to something so unspeakable.

Am I guilty by association? Do the others realize I was the last person to see Toby before he did what he did? As if sharing a car ride made me an accessory to his crime. As if being friends with the wrong person made me guilty, too.

But the worst thought that claws at my stomach

isn't about what the others believe. It's that maybe they are right.

I should have known. Should have seen it. Should have called him out when his temper flared instead of trying to distract him.

How could I be so close to someone... and not notice he was unraveling?

And if I missed that, what else have I missed? What else was hiding in people's smiles and silences? Should I be looking at my friends with suspicion every time someone acts a little different?

Earlier, I saw Alyssa's splotchy face and swollen eyes. I heard she is having a tough time with this too. But I still haven't cried. Not yet.

Because of Toby, I will never be the same again.

Twenty-Five: Toby

SEVEN MONTHS after arriving in juvie, I'm transported to a psychiatrist's office. I guess they want to see if I'm crazy.

The psychiatrist introduces himself, but I don't remember his name because I'm not looking to make friends here. He asks me dumb questions like: Do I know what the day of the week is? What grade am I in? Who is the President? Do I know why I am in his office?

I begrudgingly answer his stupid questions except I tell him I don't know why I'm here. The psychiatrist explains the court is required to check my mental health to determine whether or not I will be tried as an adult.

Wait.

There's going to be a trial? Who is getting tried as

an adult? I'm confused as to why there would be a trial when I have expressed over and over I don't remember anything. How can they conduct a trial for someone who has no memory of what happened? Plus, nobody important died! She was just some dumb mail carrier who got what she had coming to her. Of course, I keep my opinion about the dead bitch to myself, for self-preservation.

The session lasts a quick hour. What was the point of dragging me all that way? As a matter of fact, I'm surprised by Dr. Whatshisname saying he will see me again the following week.

Back at Juvie the guards keep me separated from the other kids. I'm in a room to myself with two guards posted outside my cell around the clock. They seem nice enough, but they don't say much.

Suddenly, I remember I missed my last two exams and wonder if I will be required to take them during the summer. What about that English exam? Did I get a C so I can move up a grade? My friends pop into my mind. Oh man, I bet the rumor mills are running like crazy and imagine people are thinking twice about the way they treated me. Surely, I've earned their respect now.

My second session with Dr. Whatshisname isn't as calm as our first visit. He is pushing me to remember the details of the day I was arrested. He discloses the detectives found a bloody knife under my bed, in my tackle box. He asks me to explain how the knife got there. For the hundredth time, I don't know anything and I want no part of this discussion. He questions my memory, implying I might be lying. He continues to hound me for answers on the mail carrier's murder. He repeatedly claims I in fact do remember, but I refuse to admit to the memory.

The doctor's allegations infuriate me. He is very brave to be so brazen toward me. The dam of my furor bursts and I scream at him to shut the fuck up. The smug look on his face causes me to reign in my temper before I lose complete control.

For a minute there, Dr. Whatshisname almost met The Savage. Of course, I still haven't heard from The Savage so maybe the doctor gets a pass for now. But I picture my hands squeezing his neck until his life drains from his eyes as a guard loads me into the transport van.

At our third and final session a guard stands in the corner of Dr. Whatshisname's office. He probably ratted me out and convinced someone he is suddenly scared of me. His voice is quiet and controlled as he repeats the same questions and I repeat the same answers. Why must we do this dance?

After he's finished asking the routine questions, the

doctor inquiries about my daily habits. His revelation of having met with my parents unnerves me. I feel my eyes bulge as he divulges his knowledge of my past transgressions. Hearing him describe the details of the two women on the side of the road sends a heaviness through my core. I break out in a cold sweat when he asks me what happened to the librarian's yard. My stomach lurches. I'm caught.

I tell him the parts I remember. I explain how and why I attacked the librarian's yard. I confess to stopping those two women on the side of the road at night. In a failed attempt to divert his attention away from the mail carrier's death, I admit to making obscene phone calls as a way to relieve pent up stress.

Dr. Whatshisname remains obsessed with my lack of memory surrounding the day of my arrest. I tell him I remember seeing the mail carrier whenever she delivered our mail, but I don't remember what she looked like. Maybe by admitting to a handful of events, I can appease his curiosity.

Besides, I didn't kill her. She got herself killed by The Savage in retaliation for her lack of cooperation.

He still won't believe me.

The conversation switches gears as he attempts to check in on my emotions. I vent to him, explaining I'm sad. I want to go home to my parents and my cat. My voice quivers as I detail the burden of attorney expenses my parents are facing. I also disclose how they are upset with the accusations and my behavior toward them during visitations. I want to stop their suffering. I express my bewilderment over remaining at the detention center. Why is no one allowing me to go home?

"Toby, you acknowledge your parents are hurt by your actions?"

"Yes, doctor, I know they're hurt."

"Can you acknowledge your exact actions?"

"I don't understand the question."

"Toby, I am referring to the actions that got you arrested on June 2nd."

"I do not know what actions you're talking about. I did not do anything wrong on June 2nd."

"Toby, you killed a woman on June 2nd. You stabbed her at least 60 times and you slit her throat. You ran back home where you were later arrested."

"Stop saying these lies! I went home after school and fell asleep. Nothing else happened!"

I refuse to answer any more of his stupid questions. I ask the guard to take me back to Juvie. I don't want to see Dr. Whatshisname ever again.

Within a week, I'm transferred to the county jail. My attorney notifies me I will be charged with homicide and will be housed and tried as an adult. I will not be going home to my parents any time soon. And I won't be returning to Juvie.

After two weeks in county jail, I contemplate my options and request my attorney arrange a meeting to include my parents. I am resolute to spare my family from the social embarrassment and financial drain of a trial. Confessing is my only option according to some of the older residents of the jail. According to my attorney, the alternative is the death penalty. He explains a confession will cancel the trial in front of a jury. If admitting to the crime means my parents will be left alone, then I am willing to give the attorneys what they want.

Secretly, I will carry my denial of committing murder on the mail carrier. I know I did not kill her. The Savage knows I did not kill her. And Dr. Whathisname knows because I told him I did not kill anyone on June 2nd. My plan is to serve a small amount of time in jail and eventually go home.

Acrid bile pools in my throat as I choke on the words. My parents are blindsided by my willingness to relieve them of their financial responsibility. The solution is not ideal, but I am willing to tell them what they want to hear. I conjure answers to the questions I have been asked a million times since my arrest. My eyes dart back and forth as my voice cracks under the weight of my declaration of guilt. I admit to my audience I did the killing. Step by step, I walk them through the day of June 2nd, according to what was revealed by the police during my multitude of interviews.

Mom winces and whimpers throughout my telling. She should control her feelings. My parents leave looking dumbfounded as they shuffle down the hall to the parking lot. They appear as if they've aged a decade in front of my eyes. Their hugs are long and tight before they depart, but the embraces are given in silence.

Twenty-Six: Georgia

MY EYES FLASH OPEN; I am standing in the church yard among a patch of tall lanky pine trees. I watch my attacker kill me.

I see myself, curled and on my side. I stare into my own eyes as the light in them fades like the sun setting on Mack's tobacco crops on a cool southern evening. I hear my last breaths coming from the body in the dirt. I witness myself fading into death.

My demise repels me to an expanse with no space or time. Like a diaphanous veil floating on the wind, the weight and mass of my physical form no longer tether me to earth. My senses are overloaded, but in the most majestic way. Upon my physical passing I feel more alive than ever in my life. I assume I am transitioning to heaven.

The scents of lavender and Momma's chocolate cake envelope me like a cloak, lifting me as I ascend. The comforting aromas caress my skin as if they're part of my being. In this new place, the colors are not the same. The unfamiliar hues are extraordinarily vibrant and sharp. The tones tickle me, seeping warmth straight to my soul, making me feel giddy.

Walking through a field of the richest greens and purples reflected by endless stalks of lavender, a stunning white chapel at the edge of the meadow rises on the bright horizon. The whitewashed clapboards emulate the untainted downy feathers of doves' wings, radiating immaculate white. The intricate gossamer panes of the windows reflect a kaleidoscope of colorful luminescence. The patterns in the panes of each window fascinate me. As I move closer, images on the windows come into focus. The stained glass is a depiction of my life story, artfully rendered with the emotions of each happy scene.

Gazing back at me are imagery of past pets, my parents, my husband, and every beautiful soul I encountered in my life.

Ambient light spills from the doors as I push them open. Expecting to see a band of angels, I am taken aback to recognize this is my church where I was baptized and attended bible school, sang in the choir, and married my husband. This church is my home and will be the final resting place for my body.

Outside in the well-groomed cemetery is where Mack and Momma will lay flowers on my birthdays and remember me, but this is not where I'll be.

I won't be anchored to my headstone because I will be free. A spectator at my own funeral, my spirit floats in the rafters and gazes down.

All my loved ones gather alongside co-workers, friends, and friends of friends. Some faces are more familiar than others, but I am happy to see them lining the pews. Atticus is curled by Mack's feet at the front of the chapel. How lucky am I to behold all the people in my life gathered in one place remembering me and comforting each other!

During the funeral, I search for the people I'm closest to. On drifting footsteps, I stand beside each of them and try to inhale their essence to soothe me on my journey. Lightly touching their shoulders to comfort them and leave my imprint on them like fairy dust to remember me by.

A procession forms and my loved ones follow my coffin through the front of the church into the golden sunshine.

Gratitude and the deepest love guide me in the opposite direction.

They say goodbye to my body without me because my heavenly journey continues. Gliding toward the back of the church, I see a vaguely familiar face. Olive, who attended vacation bible school with my sister, is at the end of the procession.

As we pass each other, Olive stops and looks right at me. Our eyes lock and I swear she sees me.

Sudden fear fills her eyes. Instinctively, I place my hand on her shoulder for comfort and my energy transfers chills to her arm. The moment is fleeting; I drift outside through the back door.

Instead of seeing the tall pines usually surrounding my little country church, I find myself gazing upon an endless field of tall, bright sunflowers swaying in the breeze. Luminous golden yellows and vivid greens stretch beyond my vision into the fading horizon.

As I near the field, the swaying stalks of flowers turn into an infinity of people, waving me toward them. Hundreds of past generations of relatives await me.

Eagerly, I race toward my grandmother's waiting embrace, immediately surrounded by my ancestors as they welcome me home. Heaven is beyond what I could ever imagine because there are no earthly words to describe this place.

Twenty-Seven: Olive

I WENT on my England trip after my Junior year, lazed my way through summer preceding my Senior year, and graduated from The Academy in 1983. Beneath my tan lines and yearbook scribbles, questions lingered like ghosts at the edge of every thought:

Does Toby ever think of me and our classmates? Did my canceling our plans trigger the murder? Or, was I the original intended target? If I visited him in prison, would he look me in the eye and confess he planned to hurt me the same way he did Georgia that afternoon in June 1982?

Shame and anxiety prevented me from confronting the monster who hid from me all those years. I never discussed Toby throughout my adulthood, but I never stopped questioning what went wrong and if I missed signs along the way. In my mind I played the memories over and over again almost involuntarily.

At one of our class reunions, my friend Darcy and I reconnected. She built a solid career as a Clerk of Court in the Richmond, VA, area. We both expressed how strange it was no one seemed to be curious enough to mention Toby or the fact we grew up in the company of an insidious monster. During our conversation, Darcy explained the process of making an official FOIA (Freedom of Information Act) request to the court for trial and other legal files.

The following Monday, I sent my request and nervously awaited the files. A month later, my husband became quite curious upon retrieving the mail. A fat, overflowing envelope was delivered addressed to me from the Clerk of Court in Southampton County, VA.

I matter-of-factly told him this was the court file of evidence detailing how a friend of mine in our Junior year of high school murdered a mail carrier one day after school. At first, he laughed, assuming I was joking.

I let him marinate in the dense silence of the room until he plopped heavily onto his recliner with a thud. A slower, disbelieving laugh escapes the corners of his mouth. The unforgettable memories flowed from my mouth as I narrated the story as I knew it —the story I thought I left in the past.

Four weeks passed before I summoned the courage to open the file which would fill in the blanks for me. I couldn't bear reading a statement indicating the reason he committed murder was because I made him mad by breaking our study plans. I was terrified to see an official document stating I caused an innocent woman to lose her life. What I read in the file left me gob smacked.

Thumbing through the packet, I discovered a clump of papers marked, "Caution: Crime scene and autopsy photographs."

My skin pricked as I handed the clump to my husband, requesting he shred them immediately. I wanted to remember Georgia from an untainted time, instead of what she looked like on her most dreadful day.

The second stack included a transcript from the court. My interest piqued as I uncovered the testimony of Dr. Bombay, a renowned psychiatrist who practiced in the juvenile justice system and was an expert on predictive behaviors in youth offenders.

The transcript read like a psychological thriller. But this wasn't fiction. I had the vivid memories to prove it.

I kept reminding myself they were describing my former friend. My Toby.

Dr. Bombay conducted several clinical visits with

Toby. First, to determine his competence to stand trial. Second, to determine if Toby was legally insane at the time of the commission of the murder and kidnapping. The first time they met was in December of 1982, seven months after the horrific day.

During their meeting Dr. Bombay determined Toby to not be suffering from any deep-seated psychotic ailments. No schizophrenia. No delusions.

Toby's reactions indicated to Dr. Bombay anger, isolation, and withdrawal. The doctor detected cold, hard rage. Toby denied having any memory of the events from June 2, 1982.

Dr. Bombay went on to say in his estimation Toby possessed substantial difficulties containing his sexual impulses and most likely was engaged in forceable rape at the time of the murder. Being pressed further involving his memory triggered Toby into a rage in the doctor's office, threatening bodily harm to Dr. Bombay. Throughout their meetings Toby admitted to stopping the two women on the highway as well as making obscene phone calls to the female church members. He also admitted to desecrating the librarian's yard.

Dr. Bombay stated each of these incidents occurred after a rageful event. In the case of Toby, the rage pushed him into initiating a vengeful plan.

And then came the line that cracked my spine with

dread: "By the time he implemented his plan, he was no longer in a state of rage."

It wasn't impulsive. It wasn't blind fury. It was deliberate and organized. Cold and calculated. Chills consumed me as flashes of "dark Toby" came flooding back from my childhood.

In my mind, I presumed during moments of rage Toby became a violent monster. To consider him methodical and in control while he executed his devious plans was virtually too much to comprehend.

Toby was a real Dr. Jekyll and Mr. Hyde.

This clinical description of a childhood friend left me speechless, cringing, and caused my head to spin but I couldn't stop reading. I was equally repulsed and spellbound. Dr. Bombay's testimony punched me in the face and at times made my scalp run hot from shame for Toby. How did I miss the signs? I assumed our friendship ran deep. I thought I knew the entire, real Toby, however, I did not. I curled into myself, shivering under the weight of this realization.

I continued reading as I mentally retreated against the chill of reality. An evil being walked among us, hidden in plain sight. The boy with whom I rode home from school was a dichotomy of uncontrolled emotions yet calculated in the way he took liberties. He secretly tormented people through measured logic and organized execution. His pendulum swung from a total loss of control to hyper focused implementation of revenge.

Dr. Bombay wrote how Toby engaged in rageful reactions disproportionate to his normal interaction within the community. He referred to the characteristic as the Mask of Sanity. This is where on the surface an individual lives daily life effectively having no substantial problems in the community, and suddenly a stressful event takes place. The individual reacts and does amazingly destructive things, cools off, and comes back to grips of reality, continuing to live his/her life unremorsefully and guilt-free.

I questioned the cause of Toby's rageful reactions to sexual impulses. The doctor's assessment mentioned Toby's sexual drive and aggressive feelings being fused where normally they would separate as children mature into young adults. No remorse exists because remorse would come from the admission of wrongdoing. Toby didn't believe his behavior was wrong.

In the attack of Georgia, he violated her as an object, not a human being. Toby's assault of Georgia was not triggered by Georgia herself, rather the act was another opportunity to seek revenge against an object due to a rage induced event. The exact event is not recorded in the report, but I know exactly what the event was.

In Dr. Bombay's opinion, Toby was a danger to society. Incarceration was preferred as a protective measure to the community. No therapies or drugs were available to treat Toby's violent impulses.

He allowed his friends and family to see his shell but kept private the demon living inside. Seeing this written in an official report buckles my spine and tickles the back of my neck with fingers of terror.

This doctor described a person I did not fully know; his descriptions triggered memories I didn't want to face. I was being forced to look this monster in his eyes without his mask. I couldn't put the mask back on him, nor could I excuse his behaviors as quirky personality traits. I lost my childhood friend. I would never be able to see him in any other light except the predator he truly was. Digesting the diagnosis brought forth a swirling cyclone of emotions.

In reading the dark descriptions in the reports, I was able to absolve myself of the guilt I carried all those years. As an adult, I could clearly see that I nor my classmates possessed the capacity to reconcile Toby's character flaws as dangerous signs. Nor did we have the ability to help him be someone he wasn't. Although the boy I once knew is long gone, I can't help but feel a lingering empathy for the teenager he was trapped in the grip of urges he likely didn't understand, burdened by isolation, and silently crying out in a world that didn't seem to hear him. I often pray that during his incarceration he found even a sliver of solace. Hopefully he knew, before everything unraveled, we had genuinely valued and loved him as a friend.

I wondered if he'd ever understood his urges. If he'd ever cried when no one was looking. Did he ever wish he could be normal? Did he even realize he wasn't normal?

As I gather the papers and ease them back into the overstuffed envelope, I pause, my fingers trembling slightly. My thoughts drift to Georgia, Toby's victim. Her name was a heavy bell tolling inside me.

I remember standing in the church at her funeral, feeling her presence like a whisper against my skin. Sunlight poured through stained-glass windows, casting fractured beams across her casket.

For years, that moment has replayed in my mind: the way I thought I saw her, the unmistakable sensation that she was there. It startled me at first, a jolt of fear that made my breath catch until it was replaced by something strangely peaceful. A hush. A chill that wrapped around me like a shiver of grace.

Sunlight streamed through the stained-glass

windows that day, painting the pews with splintered light. In that sacred, trembling silence, I felt as if Georgia was passing through pausing just long enough to let us know she was on her way to someplace kinder, more radiant. For a split second, I felt her. Georgia had brushed past me just long enough to say goodbye.

I held my breath and closed my eyes. When I blinked them open, she was there. Georgia!

I saw her. And then I didn't. In that moment I knew she had moved on to someplace else. Someplace warmer and brighter and kinder. Eternal kindness is what awaited Georgia.

I'm jarred out of my fog with images I had seen in my nightmares. Images I had filled in with guesses and assumptions and newspaper articles. I can't stop imagining the sheer terror she must have felt in her final moments on that terrible, twisted route she never should've had to take.

It's in those moments of remembering that my grief sharpens into anger. I rage at what Toby became, at what he did and the horrible choices he made. He stole our innocence from us, shredding it into unsalvageable trash. But tangled in that fury is devastation for Georgia, whose life was cut brutally short, and for all who loved her. Her absence is a wound that never really closed. And yet, I also grieve for the boy I once knew as

Toby, and for his family, who lost a son not only to the justice system, but to the darkness he gave in to. They too were swallowed by the aftermath of his actions. They lost him, not to death, but to something darker. We all did.

That day left a scar on our town, our school, our graduating class. A shadow that lingers, quiet and unyielding, reminding us of what was taken, and of all that can never be returned.

A scar that reminds us: Some monsters wear familiar faces.

Say Her Name
Theresa "Terri" Brickey Brantley

W HILE THIS BOOK IS FICTIONAL, the story is based on the true murder of a young woman, Theresa "Terri" Brickey Brantley. Theresa was brutally killed on the afternoon of June 2, 1982, while delivering mail.

Theresa "Terri" earned a degree in Recreation Administration from Radford College. Theresa was a member of the Radford College band. She attended Pinegrove Assembly of God in Windsor, VA, where she directed the Youth of Christ's Ambassadors Group. She worked as a rural relief mail carrier. She was a loving wife, daughter, sister, granddaughter, and friend whose life was snuffed out at the age of 24.

Her killer, Rodney Scott Simms, was 17 years old when he kidnapped and murdered Terri while on her mail route. He was convicted of kidnapping and murder and was sentenced to prison for life. He died in prison. He was Karen's classmate and friend from the 5th grade until he took Terri's life at the end of our Junior year.

Too frequently, victims are pushed to the background in the most important stories of their lives. As you close the pages of this book and reflect upon its story, please remember to say her name:

Terri Brantley

Acknowledgments

We would like to thank our amazing family--Noah, Darren, Sarah, and Cameron--for their unconditional love and support. Your in-your-face critiques, both good and bad, have challenged us in all the right ways, and your unwavering faith in our ability to write these stories and tell our truths has meant everything. We love you all to the moon and back times infinity!

To our countless friends who continue to cheer us on as we stumble through this creative journey--thank you. Your patience and encouragement as we "give birth" to these projects have been a lifeline. Your support keeps us moving, even on the days when the mountain seems too steep.

Finally, an enormous thank you to our Sugar Coated Murder podcast community. Your ongoing encouragement and enthusiasm inspire us to keep digging into the darkness and finding the light.

MOMMA's CHOCOLATE CAKE

Cake

1 cup **butter**, softened
1 cup **unsweetened cocoa powder**
2 ½ cups **sugar**
2 tsp **baking soda**
½ tsp **baking powder**
4 **eggs**, room temperature
½ tsp *Killa Vanilla*
½ tsp **salt**
2 ¾ cups all-purpose **flour**
2 cups **water**

Sea Foam Icing

4 **egg whites**
3 cups **brown sugar**
2 tsp *Killa Vanilla*

- Preheat oven to 350 degrees. Grease and flour 3 nine-inch round cake pans
- Mix flour, baking soda, baking powder, and salt in a bowl
- In a separate bowl, cream butter and sugar until well combined.
- Add eggs one at a time and beat well after each addition. Beat on high until light and fluffy and stir in Killa Vanilla.
- Alternate adding water and dry ingredients to the creamed mix and combine well.
- Divide mixture into 3 cake pans. Bake for 25-30 minutes until done. Cool 10 minutes in pans then flip onto a wire rack and cool completely.
- While the cakes are cooking start the icing by whisking eggs whites, brown sugar and water in the upper part of a double boiler.
- Bring water in the bottom part of the double boiler to a boil.
- Place top part on the boiler and beat mixture constantly on medium speed for 7 minutes until icing looks fluffy and forms stiff peaks.
- Remove from heat and fold in Killa Vanilla. Use the icing in between layers as well as on the sides and top.

About the Authors

Karen and Anne are sisters who grew up in a traditional family home in the 70s and 80s in Franklin, VA. They both attended colleges in Raleigh, NC—Anne at Peace College, and Karen at Meredith College— where their sisterly bond began to flourish.

They enjoy reminiscing about the quirky events of their childhood, especially their antics as teenagers in a small town. Their love of baking was born in their Momma's kitchen, and their humorous style of storytelling was honed with dark humor and a flair for the Southern dramatic

Now, they are both professionals by day and podcasters by night. Their podcast, Sugar Coated Murder, is a combination of baking, true crime, and of course dark, inappropriate humor.

.

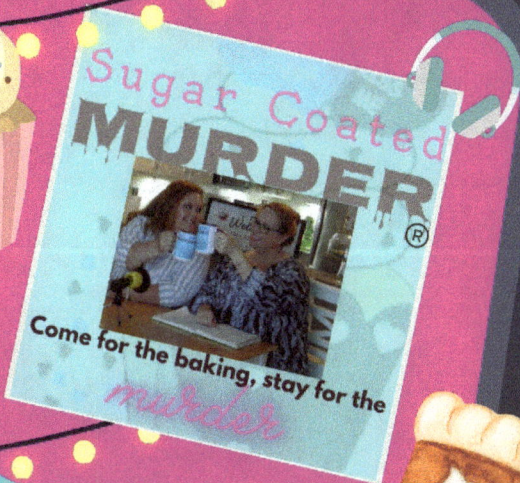

Two true crime podcast sisters get the scoop of a lifetime when they are given intimate details about a murder cover-up in their hometown. How does a small-town good-natured teenager land on a kill list? A toxic friendship out of control results in a murder. On a clear Friday night, three classmates gather. A shot rings out and one is dead, but no one knows for over two years.

This is the story of teenage rebellion gone unchecked, a deadly collaboration, and The Plan where there is no turning back once set in motion.

The dedicated podcasters shine a light on the forgotten victim and resurrect his importance in the biggest event of his young life.

CLICK CLICK CLICK

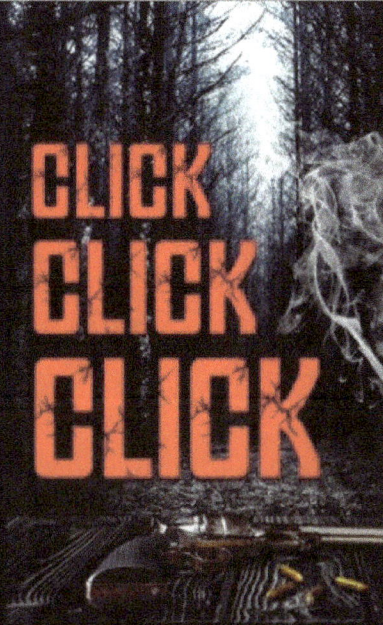

Say My Name Series

Anne Varner | Karen DeVanie

OUTSTANDING CREATOR AWARDS WINNER

PAGE TURNER AWARDS 2023 FINALIST

BIG BOOK AWARD 2023

Readers' Favorite®
Book Reviews and Award Contest

Katlyn M.
★★★★★

Gripping from start to finish!
Reviewed in the United States on N
This book had me hooke
had everything a true cr
town charm mixed with
Click is a must read for a
true crime cases. I am es

Joni West
★★★★★ Verified Purchase

ate this book up!!! The Sugar Coated Murder Podcast
sters wrote a winner!
iewed in the United States on Nove
n one of thousands of T
ar Coated M
7, 2022
s who enjoy the
hern Cooking
ue and tasty
Varner and
their...

MWO2
★★★★★ Verified Purchase

Excellent book!
Reviewed in the United States on
Loved the book!

Excellent small town story!
★★★★★ Verified Purchase
Reviewed in the United States on D
Book painted a picture of sm
All small towns have their
grew up in a small town
details but you would
processes and ends

www.ingramcontent.com/pod-product-compliance
Lightning Source LLC
Chambersburg PA
CBHW072145270326
41931CB00010B/1888